GAME DAY GLORY

LIFE-CHANGING PRINCIPLES FOR SPORT

John and Cindy White

SD Myers Publishing Services

Published by *S.D. Myers Publishing Services*
180 South Avenue
Tallmadge, OH 44278

First Printing, April 2006

Printed in the United States of America

ISBN: 0-939320-07-X

Cover Design: Dave Huff
Production Artist: Jeanette Kilchenman
Project Editor: Cynthia Berry
Production Manager: Gina Burk

To learn more about this book go to **www.gamedayglory.com**
Requests for information should be addressed to:
John White
Athletes In Action
651 Taylor Dr.,
Xenia, OH 45385
e-mail requests to: **info@gamedayglory.com**

Kingdom Living in Sport Series

This resource is a collaborative effort through the Sport Ethics Department of Athletes in Action. This department was recently founded to address and to engage the "big issues" in sport from a holistic, Christian perspective. With you, we desire sport to be a slice of life where sportsmanship and competitive excellence are shared convictions in how a Christian athlete and coach competes–a Kingdom approach to sport.

"Come help change the way we think,
feel and do sport for the glory of God."

"Athletes in Action's years of experience in sports ministry and practical field application have resulted in these biblical principles for competition, a series of studies that is truly life changing."

Frank Reich, President, Reformed Theological Seminary-Charlotte
Retired NFL Quarterback

"How one competes in sports can say a lot about what drives that person from the inside. God created us for the purpose of knowing and worshipping Him. We're to submit our hearts, and our very lives to glorifying the One who gives us life and breath, as well as our abilities and opportunities. This study will help us focus on glorifying God in all that we experience through sports in order to have a very unique opportunity to develop, demonstrate and express many of the attributes of our Heavenly Father. And I'd like to think that makes God smile."

Clark Kellogg, TV Analyst for CBS Basketball
Retired NBA Player

"Game Day Glory profoundly addresses the exciting and sometimes difficult walk of a Christian athlete. We live in a day when every other athlete on television 'thanks God' during a post-game interview. But is that all God wants from us–a half-hearted post game thank you? What you do on the playing field is a direct reflection of God. Sports can become a strong and vital part of your Christian walk. This book shows you how and gets you focused on what is REALLY important in sports."

Shannon Kurek, Principal, HFP Racing

"I played softball in the Olympics but it wasn't until I learned and applied these principles that I became a 'total' athlete - physical, mental and spiritual. I learned that God had me on the field for a purpose and that I needed to allow others to see God through my performance and trust Him when I was feeling like a failure."

Leah O'Brien-Amico, USA Softball
Olympic Gold Medalist 1996, 2000, 2004

"The biblical principles, insights and practical applications included in *Game Day Glory,* if followed, will transform the people of sport on and off the playing fields and courts. The connections outlined in each chapter challenge the reader to interconnect belief and behavior with the hope of transforming the way sport is played and valued."

Valerie Gin, Gordon College Professor, Former Volleyball Coach

"The principles in this book help give you the proper perspective of your sport. I really enjoyed learning how to be motivated by my relationship with Jesus Christ. I still try to apply them, and God continues to show me the areas of my life that I need to surrender to Him."

Richard Jefferson, New Jersey Nets, 2004 Olympic Team

"The principles in *Game Day Glory* encourage athletes to compete in a way that trusts God's power rather than leaning on their own strength. It's not about the fans, your family, your coaches, or the wins. It's about having that one desire to play and bring glory to the Lord, your Audience of One."

Tanisha Wright, Seattle Storm (WNBA)

"Through my experience with the AIA principles outlined in this book, I have learned to put Christ at the center of my life everyday. I have also learned how to play for His glory. What I do with my talent is my gift to God because He is the only one who gives me strength in all that I do."

Roger Evenson, Chicago Cubs

"The principles in this book helped me to bring honor and glory to the Lord Jesus by giving me greater motivation than so many of the other things that had driven me to train and compete hard. In the Montreal Olympics, in 1976, I was given an opportunity to apply this thinking. The pressure of competing in front of millions of people began to leave. As I went out on the mat to wrestle to the best of my ability, I could focus on wrestling for the Lord Jesus."

John Peterson, USA Wrestling
Olympic Silver Medalist, 1972, Olympic Gold Medalist, 1976

"*Game Day Glory* allowed me to see that God had given me a gift in playing football and it was to honor Him. Worshiping Him through my performance was my way of saying 'thank you,' even through injury and adversity. My performance was at a much higher level because I knew that the one person I was going to be pleasing was the Lord. That was my main focus, and I continue to live that way in my retirement. When people look at me, I know they will see the football player, but hopefully, and more importantly, they will see Jesus in and through me."

Anthony Munoz, NFL Hall of Fame Offensive Tackle, Class of 1998
Named to the NFL's 75th Anniversary Team

"When I went to an AIA summer camp as a sophomore in college and learned the principles in *Game Day Glory* for the first time, it was life-changing. As I learned to be more Christ-centered and glorifying through athletics, a major activity of my life became more connected to the most important, foundational aspect of who I was–my relationship with Jesus."

Dr. Erik Thoennes, Associate Professor of Biblical Studies and Theology,
Talbot School of Theology and Biola University

"These spiritual principles remind us that we should be more focused, more competitive and more patient in competition."

Greg Ryan, Head Coach Men's Volleyball,
University of Calgary

"It was so cool to apply the principles in this book to my sport–but as I got involved in everyday life I realized this should be required teaching for every human being in any vocation. They revolutionized my life in the way I look at sports and life."

Josh Davis, Swimmer, 3-time Gold Medalist

"As youth coaches, we have an opportunity to have an impact on the lives of children by providing an environment that stresses the importance of good, godly sportsmanship. *Game Day Glory* gives us the principles needed to teach these children the proper behavior on and off the field and the first way we do this is to lead by example."

Shawn Brown, Youth Soccer Director and Coach,
CJ United Soccer Club

"*Game Day Glory* provides the highly trained athlete, as well as the competitive recreational participant with an opportunity to truly and deeply explore his or her perspectives and motivations for competing while maintaining a primary focus on God. It is a rich resource for better understanding how to make faith and sport an inseparable part of the competitors' experience, in and out of the arena, thereby worshipping and honoring God. It must be part of the library of coaches, athletes, sport administrators, and sport and recreation faculty."

Paul R. Milton, Ph.D., Director, Recreation Services, Kent State University
Editor, NIRSA *Recreational Sports Journal*

Foreword

Sports are about preparation, rules, intensity, wins and losses, ups and downs, relationships and a right perspective. Many people leave God out of sports, as if He can be turned on and off whenever it is convenient or beneficial. I believe that whatever we're doing–whether we are participating in athletics or working in our garden–we are doing it in the presence of God. If I am aware of His presence in all arenas of life, it's not going to change when I hit the basketball floor, the practice floor, or the weight room; God will always be the first order of business in my mind. He is the one I want to please with my attitude, character, and actions–as a person and as a coach.

This Bible study guide will help you understand that God is your ultimate audience, the One who desires your focus and attention, even in competition. There is so much pressure to please everyone: coaches, fans, parents, and media. You won't have to worry about meeting everyone else's expectations if you desire to honor and glorify God in everything you think, say and do. You can trust the results to Him.

We are dealing with peoples' lives and we have the opportunity to show them how to live through difficult times with stability and purpose because of our relationship with the Lord. During the ongoing, adversarial situations in the competitive world of sports, you will learn to trust His promises and live with a certain joy and peace. He promises to continue His work of perfecting contentment and godliness in your life. The life-changing principles for sport, if practiced, will not only affect the way you approach competition but the way you live the rest of your life for the glory of God.

Lorenzo Romar, Head Men's Basketball Coach, Washington Huskies
Retired NBA Player

Acknowledgements

Many thanks to the Athletes in Action staff family we have been privileged to be a part of for so many years. The need for integration of faith and sports started years ago with our early leaders and continues today. A special thanks to those leaders who have paved the way: Wendel Deyo, Mark Householder, Bill Pugh, Jeff Prior, Jeff Patton and Doug Gotcher. Also, thanks to those leaders who helped to shape the principles we have today: John Hardie, Ed Uszynski, Natalie Nuce, Judy Kirkpatrick, Shauna Stone, Paula Pugh, Sherie Green, Jerry Dendinger, Suzy Hermes, Billy Crossan, Charity Bonfiglio, Aaron Mascaro, Dave Huff, Scott Huck and our interns, Chad Almy, Todd Beall and Ben McKain. We can't say thank you enough for all of the staff who have embraced and taught these principles at our summer camps and overseas tours. Your example of faith-works has changed many lives.

A special thank you to our brothers and sisters at Central State University and Wilberforce University for showing us a holistic perspective toward life and ministry. We now live and speak with a deep concern for social justice. Our time there is one of our fondest memories in ministry.

We would not be at this point without the long-term interest and faithful support of Gina Burk-Myers and Kim Nero, who prodded us along to make these life-changing principles available to the public. Thanks to Scott Myers of S.D. Myers Publishing Services and for the initial investment to get these published. And Cindy Berry, thanks for the long hours and late nights of editing.

Our children, Jonathan, Estie and Hannah, have endured more conversations about good character and ethics in sports than they ever asked for. We want to say to them and all those we have taught–thanks for trusting that it is best to live out God's kingdom principles amidst the challenges we face in sports today.

Last, our gratitude to God is immeasurable. He has called us both from the "dominion of darkness and brought us into the kingdom of the Son he loves, in whom we have redemption, the forgiveness of sins" (*Col. 1:13, 14, NIV*). God has given us great purpose, peace and passion so that we may help others work out their salvation in the world of sports. To Him be the Glory!

To the Athletes in Action staff family
and all of the young athletes and coaches
who desire to compete with purpose, integrity, joy and honor.

Preface

We grew up as youngsters racing our friends, swimming in ponds, hot-dogging down Midwestern ski slopes (if that is possible), playing backyard games of football, baseball and dodgeball and losing ourselves in those dreams where you shoot the game winning shot and make it every time!

We loved sports so much that after graduating from those elementary experiences, we went on to compete in high school championships, national championships in college, international competitions, and coach in college and at the United States Olympic Training Center (Developmental Program).

We learned so much about life in our sport experiences: discipline, personal responsibility, loyalty, cooperation, losing with honor, winning with humility, and setting and meeting goals. It was glorious!

But the glory of sport is fading. We are saddened by the countless athletes and coaches we counsel who have lost all sense of value and purpose because they are just part of a big machine called "sport." Their whole existence is validated or nullified by their win-loss record. The pressure is too great; the joy is gone. They are in bondage to success, fame, power and money and don't know how to make life work in this intense world.

We are angered by those ugly moments that are all too frequent in competition reminiscent of the gladiatorial age: vicious cheap shots, purposeful injury, shameless cheating, and physical and emotional abuse. And it is not just at the collegiate and professional level. As youth coaches, we have watched a girl's soccer league expel six-and seven-year-old players from the game because of foul language and cheap shots! This year, in our "Christian" basketball league, we had to play against a coach who cheated to win and justified it in the name of the game. We are not too far away from the case in Alabama where a little-league coach alledgedly paid a player to throw a ball at the face of a mentally challenged teammate during warm-ups so that he wouldn't be able to participate in the play-off game.

We really don't want to lose the glory of the game. Sport is too good to watch it fade away without a serious attempt to bring positive change. Rick Reilly of *Sports Illustrated* said that it is time to "ask more probing questions about sport." Even years before us, Frank Deford, another *Sports Illustrated* writer, tackled these critical issues by asking Christian sport ministries what they felt their role was in confronting the persistent social problems (e.g., racism, sexism, cheating, brutality, etc.) of sport. Sadly, he concluded in his many interviews that, "Not one even remotely suggested any direct effort was being considered to improve the morality [ethics] of athletics."

Whether this is actually true, we are not sure. There are serious attempts being made by many sporting institutions to raise the level of moral conduct in sport. We also understand that not everyone shares the same values in sport and education, especially at a higher level. That is why we have developed a curriculum to keep winning important, while raising the bar for character and godliness for those who desire to bring glory to God in competitive sports.

For over 20 years, being staff members of Athletes in Action, we have equipped many college and professional athletes to compete in a way that honors God. But what does that mean? How do you do that? Can you be intense and still be a Christian? Is winning a good goal? How do I sort out my motivations to please my coach, my parents and my friends? Is God glorified if I am injured or not starting? Why do I get so angry when we lose? How can I keep sports in perspective with all of my other priorities? These are good questions, and *Game Day Glory* will help you understand sport from a Christian worldview.

The principles in this book have been tested and implemented for years and we felt that it was time to make them available to you. We are educators at heart so you will discover not only theological and biblical insight but practical application for every principle. Coaches, parents and athletes can learn and apply these principles so that what we believe can show up in how we behave. Who knows–maybe if we work harder at bridging that gap, the glory of sport will be restored for the glory of God.

John and Cindy White
On the eve of youth basketball tournaments and March Madness

Contents

Introduction

Christians involved in sports often have difficulty knowing how their relationship with Christ relates to their sport. If a collegiate student-athlete or professional wants to take her faith seriously, she faces several tough questions: What should be my motivation in competition? Should I pray before a game? Should I pray for victory? Should I put a cross or verse on my sweatband? How should I relate to my coaches, teammates, and opponents? How do I know that God wants me to devote hours each day to my sport when I could be on the mission field? What differentiates competition that pleases God from that which doesn't please God? What does God have to do with game day?

> *"Sport has the power to change the world. It has the power to unite people in a way that little else does."*
> Nelson Mandela

All of these are complex questions; there are no easy answers. As one person put it, "For every difficult question there's a simple answer...and it's usually wrong." The same is true in learning to approach athletic competition from a Christian perspective. There are a variety of "simple solutions" most of which only superficially address the issue of faith and sports. For instance, some people view God as a lucky rabbit's foot that will help us win the game (a justification for a "pre-game chapel"). Some people relegate God to the sideline by making their faith a private thing ("this is competition; my faith is for Sunday or my small group Bible study"). Some Christians can so fuse their faith with their sport that their desires, interests, and feelings are projected upon God. In fact, in some cases, Christians approach sports no differently than non-Christians.

> *"The unexamined athlete and coach are not worth competing."*
> (Socrates quote, "The unexamined life is not worth living," applied to sports)

Simply putting a cross on one's sweatband, praying before or after a competition or thanking God for a victory on national television pales in comparison to how God wants to transform our athletic competition into an instrument for worship. The God of the Bible is not a Santa Claus we can use to get what we want, nor is He a chump that we can keep safely at arm's length. Neither is He just an "addendum" that we can tack onto our lives. Instead, God wants to transform all areas of our lives by revolutionizing the way we understand ourselves and our role in His Kingdom.

"There is not a square inch in the whole domain of human existence over which Jesus Christ, who is sovereign over all, does not cry, 'Mine!'"
Abraham Kuyper, former Dutch Prime Minister

Purpose of the Study

The intent of this Bible study is to challenge you to rethink your involvement in and perspective on sport. These studies are designed to renew, challenge and transform your perspective, motivation, character, response, and priorities in the world of competitive sport as followers of Christ. Because we are created in God's image, we believe sport should be a God-ward activity, worship. Our participation on game day honors or glorifies God by demonstrating mutual respect for others toward the goal of excellence. For a Christian athlete, coach, administrator or fan, excellence is exhibited by competitiveness, celebration and character. How you the play the game does matter! In the spirit of Eric Liddell, as dramatized in the movie, *Chariots of Fire*, we desire for you to run, swim, block, dribble and compete in such a way that "you feel God's pleasure."

We want to ask you to have the courage to reflect deeply about your own motivation for competing as an athlete and a coach. We want to ask you to hold your life and your sport with an open hand so that God can be Lord of your sport and your life–an (Audience of One).

"It is a fitting occasion to give thanks to God for the gift of sport, in which the human person exercises his body, intellect and will, recognizing these abilities as so many gifts of his Creator."
Pope John Paul II

Structure of the Study

This study has a basic outline that allows for flexibility and purposefulness to meet your personal and small group needs. Each lesson is designed to take approximately 60 to 90 minutes to complete individually, but potentially longer when you factor in such group dynamics as spiritual maturity, relationship building, and sensitivity to God's leading. To thoroughly cover each section, we suggest that you take 2-3 weeks per study section (a semester for the entire study book). However, if time is limited, then please lead with creativity and freedom. We suggest you allow each person to review the study in advance so some prep work is done before the group meets, decide which questions (in advance) are most important for the overall purpose of the study and your group needs, or give each person some devotional work that could be followed-up one-on-one. Finally, realize that this is a process or journey so you might have to revisit this another time.

There are multiple connections for each chapter:

CONTEMPORARY CONNECTION: A relevant bridge to connect your group with the overall topic and theme of the study.

HISTORICAL CONNECTION: Cultural background information, concepts, and some explanatory commentary to serve as a reference for your study.

BIBLICAL CONNECTION: The actual story from the Bible that you will observe, interpret and apply for each specific study.

SPORT CONNECTION: Centers the discussion and addresses the application to the people and culture of competitive sports.

- **Putting it Together (JUST BE IT and JUST DO IT):** Offers practical tips on how you can integrate your faith and sport (practicing God's presence) in a moment-by-moment reality of practice and competition.

GOD CONNECTION: Expands your view of God in a practical and experiential way.

DAILY CONNECTION: Daily exercises that can deepen these principles in your walk with God for sport and life.

Reminders: Summarizes the main points of the study.
Notes and Resources: For further research.
For Further Study/Reflection/Application: Provides the option to go beyond the study for deeper interaction and application of the theme. You are asked to use some Bible reference resources. If you do not have these, ask some one at your church, a friend, a bookstore or see http://bible.crosswalk.com.
Quotations: Reflection and conversation-starters that complement each section of the study.

Practical Outline

PRINCIPLE ONE - **Audience of One**

GOD owns you and your sport

Passage: *1 Kings 18:20-40 "The Story of Elijah & the Prophets of Baal"*

Theme 1: God exposes our idols, changing our allegiance from "substitutes" to Him so that sport is an instrument for worship.

Practice: Competing in sports as an opportunity for worship, a (thank-you response).

PRINCIPLE TWO - **Inside Game**

GOD's love is the maximum motivation

Passage: *Luke 15:11-32 "The Story of the Prodigal Son"*

Theme 2: Our identity in Christ frees us to compete with a "grace motivation."

Practice: Breaking the cycle of the performance-trap by remembering God's truth.

PRINCIPLE THREE - **Holy Sweat**

GOD provides resources for spiritual training to cultivate Christlike character

Passage: *Luke 4:1-13 "The Temptation of Jesus"*

Theme 3: Maturity is the process of God's Spirit growing us in grace 'over time' through the spiritual disciplines that cultivate Christlike habits and character traits.

Practice: Taking fundamental truths into competition through focal points.

PRINCIPLE FOUR - **Hurtin' for Certain**

GOD allows pain and trials to deepen your character for Him

Passage: *Genesis 37-50 "The Story of Joseph"*

Theme 4: Trials and suffering are part of God's game for molding and shaping us, as we see and respond appropriately.

Practice: Seeing pain in sports and life as a training ground for developing character.

PRINCIPLE FIVE - **Victory Beyond Competition**

GOD's playing field extends beyond your competition

Passage: *Matthew 25:14-30 "The Parable of the Talents"*

Theme 5: The return of the King calls us to be faithful stewards of our time, talents and treasures, now in sports, as well as beyond.

Practice: Transforming every area of life into kingdom living.

(*Definition of Principles for Sport:* 1. Basic beliefs and commitments. 2. A vision for and of sports. 3. A guide for how we ought to live in sports.)

"Many people think church is the only place to worship God. But you can worship God no matter where you are or what you're doing. A soccer field is one of my favorite places to worship. Before the national anthem, I pray my performance will bring glory to God. Then the field becomes my church [sanctuary], and playing to the best of my ability, a form of praise."
(Cat Reddick, US National Women's Soccer Team, UNC Women's Soccer)

One hundred thousand fans screaming and waving, ESPN televising, your mom wincing, dad stressing, friends cheering, the cameras zooming, and your opponent strutting, rocks your soul with charged emotion for this phenomenon appears to be "more than a game." You know all too well how this experience can affect your focus, performance, and the outcome of the game itself. Who doesn't love the attention and applause as you finish or make the game-winning goal or basket? How are competitors absorbed in this excitement-filled drama suppose to make sense of the multiple audiences that either honor or condemn us for our efforts?

Human beings fundamentally are spiritual beings longing to worship something or someone. Sometimes we settle for less than the highest object of worship. As C. S. Lewis, author of "The Weight of Glory," said, "We are far too easily pleased." If you are a Christian, that someone you are privileged to know and worship is God Himself. He is our Audience in the sense that we do life, sports and work ultimately "in" or "before" His presence (literally, His face). However, He is not like a cheering, fanatic spectator waiting to see who wins. Instead, God is our loving Father-always present-intimately concerned with all that we do in life as His children, even our play on game day.

Let's take the ceiling off of our audience-packed arenas and discover an amazing Audience who is in, around, and with us as our quads burn and mouths thirst. God wants you to be deeply connected with Him so that your sport is a sacred means to worship Him–even on fourth and one.

P|1
C|1

1 Chapter

PRINCIPLE ONE

1 Kings 18:20-40 "The Story of Elijah & the Prophets of Baal"

Audience of One

GOD OWNS YOU AND YOUR SPORT

God exposes our idols, changing our allegiance from "substitutes" to Him so that sport is an instrument for worship.

Audience of One

CONTEMPORARY CONNECTION:

1. Describe a memorable moment in your athletic experience that you will always remember (the sights, sounds, place, event, people). How old were you? Why was this so significant for you? Can you relate to Arthur Ashe's quote? Why or why not?

2. Look below in the box through the list of quotes. Can you identify with any of these statements? How do these quotes compare to your memorable experience in Q.1?

> "You are nothing until you are number one" ... "No pain, no gain" ... "You don't win silver, you lose gold" (Nike Ad) ... "Without sport, weekends would be weekdays" (ESPN) ... "Second place is the first loser" ... "It's only a game when you win. When you lose it's hell" ... "Defeat is worse than death, because you have to live with defeat"

"Sports are wonderful; they can bring you comfort and pleasure for the rest of your life. Sports can teach you so much about yourself, your emotions and character, how to be resolute in moments of crisis and how to fight back from the brink of defeat. In this respect, the lessons of sports cannot be duplicated easily; you quickly discover your limits but you can also build self-confidence and a positive sense of yourself. Never think of yourself as being above sports."

(Arthur Ashe, Days of Grace)

3. What do these quotes say about today's culture concerning sport? How have you experienced these quotes?

Without sports, there would be no reason to get up on Sunday.

(ESPN billboard)

Sport, like other pursuits, was always meant to be an expression of our God-given abilities, our gifts, and our desires to enjoy and pursue excellence on this earth for God's honor and glory. When sport becomes all consuming, or a source for defining your value, purpose and meaning then instead of a healthy God-ward expression (**Audience of One**), it becomes an object of worship, an idol.

Reflect: Is it possible to become so obsessed with winning and sports that you put sports before God? How have you seen this communicated in sports, in your life, or in the life of someone else?

"Sports is a step away from the rule of the jungle, they're trying to move it back towards the jungle, when the strong survive and misuse the weaker in any way that they want. And that's really unfortunate for our whole system of values in our country."

(Kareem Abdul-Jabbar, during a *60 Minutes* interview)

P|1
C|1

> "I believe in the church of baseball. I've tried all the major religions and most of the minor ones. I've worshipped Buddha, Allah, Brahma, Vishnu, Shiva, trees, mushrooms, and Isadora Duncan. I know things. for instance, there are 108 beads in a Catholic's rosary and there are 108 stitches in a baseball. When I learned that, I gave Jesus a chance. But it just didn't work out between us. The Lord laid too much guilt on me. I prefer metaphysics to theology. You see, there's no guilt in baseball. And it's never boring... It's a long season and you gotta trust it. I've tried 'em all, I really have, and the only church that truly feeds the soul, day in, day out, is the church of baseball."
> (Annie Savoy in the movie *Bull Durham*)

HISTORICAL CONNECTION:

In many ways, the whole story of the Bible is about this everyday struggle between true worship (dependence on God), and false worship (dependence on something or someone other than God), a substitute for God. There was a point in Israel's history when the people of God depended on God-substitutes (Baal), idolatry. Instead of trusting in the God of their rich heritage, these people had pushed God aside and now God was *one among many* of the other pagan gods in the culture they were living in. Because of this tremendous spiritual crisis, God answered the people through the prophet Elijah. God's great love and concern for His people compelled Him to send a challenge through Elijah by bringing a drought that resulted in a famine. The economic and social challenges that accompanied this form of discipline pushed the people even further to find answers to meet their deepest needs or most ultimate concerns.

Definition of Terms

Baal - An idol. The Canaanite (Israel's neighboring people and culture) storm and fertility god. Baal was considered the powerful lord and owner of the thunderstorms. He was responsible for sending the rain to fertilize the land, resulting in a bountiful harvest of food for these farmers.

Further study:
Why are God's people experiencing these difficult times? (See 1 Kings 9.9)

The Jewish followers of God had combined features of their faith in God (Yahweh) with that of the Canaanites, evolving into a faith of many audiences (God + Baal/other things). They attached a name to nature itself instead of seeing God as the ultimate sustainer and source for their everyday needs.

Divided Kingdom - the book of 1 Kings opens with the end of David's reign and the beginning of Solomon's kingship. As kings, they were required to obediently lead God's people. The people were all united under David and Solomon. Calamity and chaos enter, however, when Solomon turns his heart away from God. Subsequently, rebellion and revolt occur among the leaders leaving the kingdom ripped in two: a Northern (Israel) and a Southern kingdom (Judah).

⤓Further study:
Look up 1 Kings 16:29-34 for a more complete description of King Ahab and Jezebel (his wife). What do you learn about this king and his religious practices?

Elijah - the beginning of a long line of prophets who spoke on behalf of God (like a prosecutor). Elijah bursts on the scene (1 Kings 17:1-2) critically charging God's people with violating their love-relationship (covenant) with God and exacting God's judgment on them.

BIBLICAL CONNECTION:
Read *1 Kings 18:20-40*

4. Who are the primary players/characters in this competitive showdown?

⤓Further study:
Cross-reference: Psalm 115:1-8; Hab.2:18-19; Jer. 10:1-5; Isaiah 44:9-20. Create a short list of ideas concerning the nature of idols.

P|1
C|1

5. List at least 5 things that you learn about Baal (the idol) and the worshippers (prophets) from observing the competitive drama in verses 25-29?

6. Why do you think these people were so invested in this idol? (See **HISTORICAL CONNECTION**)

> "...Sport has its "gods"—star and superstar athletes who, though powerless to alter their own situations, wield great influence and charisma over the masses of fans ...Sport has its shrines—the national halls of fame and thousands of trophy rooms and cases ...Sport also has its "houses of worship" spread across the land where millions congregate to bear witness to the manifestations of their faith."[1]
> (Harry Edwards, Sport Sociologist)

7. Israel turned to an idol for provision when circumstances (no rain and no food) were difficult. They sought help apart from their God by creating a god that they could control or manipulate for their own purposes and personal satisfaction. Is there a person, an activity, a relationship, or a desire/pleasure that you rely on to satisfy your deepest needs? When not God, where do you turn for help or satisfaction?

Further study: Cross-reference:Rom. 1:18-32; Gal. 5:16-24; Col. 3:5-11. Is this preoccupation with idols simply a struggle reserved for the Old Testament people of God? Look up some or all of the New Testament references: What verse(s) from above are particularly applicable to you about this issue of idolatry?

8. Based on the story and your experience, how would you define an idol?

"Whatever your heart clings to and confides in, that is really your God."
(Martin Luther)

Definition of an Idol: [2]

1) Something in your life or from this Earth that is inflated to function as a substitute for God.
2) Displacing God by putting something other than God at the center of my life in order to find love, satisfaction, purpose and meaning.
3) An idol can be a physical object, a created artifact, a possession, a person, an activity, a role, an organization, a dream, an image, an idea, a pleasure, a hero, anything that we trust in for satisfaction apart from God.

Summary:
"There are only two basic categories: the Creator [God] and the created. If we do not worship God, we will focus on something in creation and elevate it to the status of divinity. We will worship a false god. Our intrinsically religious nature will never allow us not to worship. Either we pledge ultimate allegiance to Yahweh, the only true God, or we commit ourselves to some created thing and make a god out of it. We must choose one or the other, for we cannot live without a god, and we cannot have two–at least not for long."[3]

Though we may not be bowing down or calling upon Baal today, we can often misdirect, misuse or spoil a good thing (activity) like sport to find meaning, purpose and value.

⍖Further study: Read Deut. 5:6-10; 6:4-9; Deut. 29:16-28. Should these people have known better than to have an idol? Why or Why not? At the heart of it, why were their actions wrong?

9. Pick 1-2 idols from the list on the next page. Explain how this might happen in the life of an athlete or coach.

P|1
C|1

How do they function as substitutes for God?

Which one (s) resonates most with you today?

How might you be manufacturing idols in your mind, heart and imagination?

Exposing Idols in Sport and Life [4]

Idol thoughts in your heart: Basic motivations that 'drive' and 'determine' your idolatry (Why you do what you do)

"When sporting competitions are swept away by violence, when there is injustice, fraud, eagerness for gain, economic and political pressures or discrimination, then sport is reduced to the level of a tool of power and money."[5]
(Pope John Paul II)

Power Idolatry: Life only has meaning/I only have worth if–I have power, control, mastery or manipulative influence over my eammates, the referees, the opponent, the score, my players, my body, the game, ____

Approval Idolatry: Life only has meaning/I only have worth if–I am loved, respected and praised by my coach, the fans, the media, my parents, my athletic director, my friends, the alumni, ___________

Image Idolatry: Life only has meaning/I only have worth if–I have a particular kind of physical look, body image, or _______________

Winning Idolatry: Life only has meaning/I only have worth if–I have been highly productive by achieving my goal of a win, a starting position, first place, a tournament bid, a head coaching position,____

Achievement Idolatry: Life only has meaning/I only have worth if–I am being recognized and affirmed for my accomplishments (wins, records, trophies, rewards, etc.).

Race/Culture Idolatry: Life only has meaning/I only have worth if–my race, state, team, university, country or culture is ascendant and recognized as superior.

Family/Coach Idolatry: Life only has meaning/I only have worth if–my coach, my teammates, the fans, my children, or my spouse are happy and happy with me.

Relationship Idolatry: Life only has meaning/I only have worth if–Mr. or Ms. "RIGHT" is in love with me.

Elijah was challenging the people to stop waffling back and forth (*1 Kings 18:21*) and being divided in their allegiance. He called them to decide that day whom they would serve. Are you willing to make the same choice (as far as what *ultimately* defines you as a person) between God and Sport, God and ______________________ (fill in the blank)?

P|1
C|1

To make this kind of choice means not confusing sport with God as your ultimate audience. You are not literally removing sport from your life, but you are identifying how sport has been sinfully damaged, perverted, misused and overvalued (an idol) by you and our culture. As you properly value sport as a God-given opportunity, then you can **choose** to direct your heart, mind, soul, body and behavior toward glorifying God in and through sport.

Further reflection: What is the point of drenching the sacrifice (v. 33-35)?

> "...basketball was the be-all, end-all of my existence... The problem was, basketball was just a game; but I was treating it like it was a god." (Luke Ridnour, NBA Player)

Removing the Idol:

Read *1 Kings 18:33-35, 36-39*

10. Who is the focus of Elijah's prayers in verses 36-37? Why is this important in light of the whole story and the final outcome?

Further reflection: God has always wanted devoted followers. Look up some other verses about making a critical choice of being a devoted follower: Deut. 30:15-20; Joshua 24:4-24; Matthew 6:24.

11. In Elijah's prayer request (v. 37), what is meant by "turning their hearts back again"?

12. Pathway to change: *Acts 3:19; Acts 14:14-18; Acts 17:30-31; 2 Cor. 10:3-5; 1 Thes. 1:9; 1 Jn. 1:9.* Look up some New Testament verses to help in your understanding of this important point as it relates to removing idols. How are they significant for describing how we change in order for us to have an (**Audience of One**).

⭳Further study: Gen. 35:5-7, 9-15, 21-26. What is the historical significance of the "sons of Jacob," the name "Israel," and the number "twelve" in 1 Kings 18:31-32? Why does the narrator of this story offer us these details as Elijah prepares and builds the altar?

13. How did the people respond to God's awesome display of power in verse 39? (Note: Pay attention to both their actions and words).

What is the connection between their response and the rules of the contest defined by Elijah in verse 24?

Summary:

As readers today, we probably should not expect God to answer by fire. He has, however, answered in an even more powerful and climactic way by giving His Son, Jesus Christ, as the sacrifice and payment for our sins of idolatry. God has visibly shown up in the person and life of Jesus Christ to turn us back and restore our relationship with God and others by forgiving us our sins. In the book of Romans, Paul portrays God (*Rom. 11:36*) as our source, sustainer and goal in life - (**Audience of One**). Because of who God is and His great mercy (*Rom. 12:1-2*), Paul commands us to be marked by a revolutionary kind of worship involving our whole person (all that we are and do) and our whole life (every sphere, activity, and relationship on this earth).

⭳Further study: Use a biblical background resource to better understand the significance of God answering by fire as proof of His Lordship and deity.

14. Read again the summary paragraph listed on the previous page. In what ways do you worship God? Describe what this looks like.

According to *Romans 12:1-2*, should our worship be limited to a Sunday service or singing worship songs? Why or why not?

"The gods we worship write their names on our faces; be sure of that. And a man will worship something–have no doubts about that, either. He may think that his tribute is paid in secret in the dark recesses of his heart–but it will [come] out. That which dominates will determine his life and character. Therefore, it behooves us to be careful what we worship, **for what we are worshiping we are becoming."**
(Ralph Waldo Emerson, American Author, Poet and Philosopher)

SPORT CONNECTION:

15. Historically, sport often has been associated with religion and worship. For example, at the ancient Olympics, the games were held in honor of Zeus. We are either worshiping God or falsely worshiping something else, an idol.

"Man's chief end is to glorify God, and to enjoy him forever."
(Westminster Shorter Catechism, 1647)

Using the (chart on page 35), what does it mean or look like for sport to be an opportunity for worship?

How is your worship expressed in your life and character in sport?

Share an experience when this happened for you. What is one area from the chart that you would like to grow in this year?

Putting it Together: JUST BE IT

↓**Further reflection:**
Two approaches to Sport and Life (Lunch plates): [6]

1. An athlete/coach who happens to be a Christian:

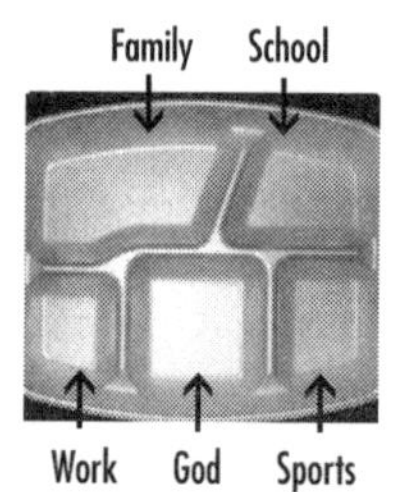

2. A Christian who happens to be an athlete/coach:

(God=whole plate)

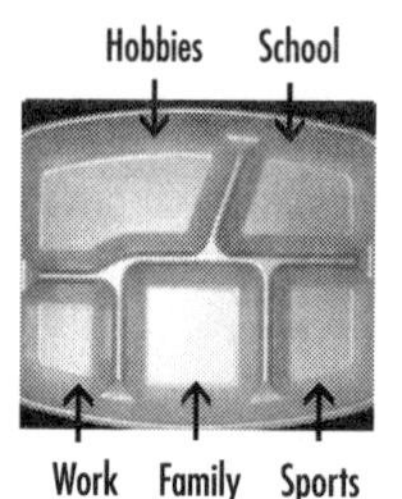

1. Describe the differences between the two approaches with respect to God and the other areas of interest.

2. Which area are you more prone to substitute for God?

3. Why?

In sport, your worship via competition is an expression of your appreciation and gratitude to God with your whole being (**Thank-You Response**). When this is true, sport serves as a mirror that reflects God's goodness, truth, love, etc. As you practice and compete you are mentally, morally, relationally, and physically thanking God and praising Him through the different ways expressed in Principle 1 (see chart on page 35).

When you practice and compete, allow your effort, intensity, regard for the game and the opponent, and respect for the coach and referees to (non-verbally) "shout" thank you to God with your whole being.

How are you thanking God today as you practice and compete? Do others know that you compete with an (**Audience of One**) by the way you worship through sports?

> "I desired to take and use that gift [God-given ability in football] to honor Him [God] through my preparation, intensity, and focus. Worshiping Him through my performance was my way of saying "thank you" to Him for specific blessings…"
> (Anthony Munoz, NFL Hall of Fame Offensive Tackle)

SPORT CONNECTION:

SPORT = IDOLS	SPORT = Audience of One (an opportunity for worship)
Use God as a "rabbit's foot"/ good-luck charm for my personal gain, win, or power.	God chooses me to image His excellent character through my effort, attitude, intensity, and sportsmanship.
Compete to prove and justify my value and worth.	God has determined my value and worth before I even compete.
Disrespect for the rules (often ignoring or breaking them) and I only abide by the rules when it is to my advantage or when I might get caught.	Compete by the rules all the time because they express what is fair, just and orderly (God's character) in order for the game to flourish.
Winning is everything and the only thing.	Competing to win consists of a serious challenge while enjoying the pursuit.
Happy when my opponent competes poorly or is hurt because my only concern is my own welfare (winning).	Believe and want the best both for my team and opponent because everyone is striving together toward excellence.
Unrealistic expectations and failure to acknowledge my physical limitations.	Accept my God-given abilities and physical limitations.
Give 100% only when those important people are watching (coach, scout, family, friends).	Give 100% both publicly and privately because God is my audience.
Do whatever it takes to win (cheat, drugs, trash-talk, etc.)= Ends justify the means.	What matters the most is how I played the game.
View the opponent as the enemy and competition like war.	View the opponent as co-competitor who deserves respect.
Celebrating victory is expressed by taunting, strutting, and entertaining because it is all about me.	Celebrating victory is expressed respectfully, appreciatively, and joyfully because it is about more than me.
Jealous of others' success because it means they are out-performing me.	Thankful for others' success because it raises my level of play and pushes us toward excellence.
See sport as a right and something I have to have in order to "make it" in life.	See competition/sport as a privilege and gift.
Unteachable spirit and disrespectful toward my coach/authority.	Teachable spirit and respectful toward my coach/authority.
Sport is my deliverer (or escape) from past poor circumstances or my family situation.	God delivers and redeems me.

GOD CONNECTION:

Worship ascribes value and worth to that which is most important in a person's life. Literally, in the Bible, the words for worship are derived from ideas that mean "kissing," "bowing," "bending" and "serving." Whatever we are worshipping will be communicated by our words, in our thoughts, through our feelings, by our choices, in our concern for others, and in our actions. Therefore, worship is embodied in everything you do (24/7). All of life is an act of worship-ascribing honor and value.

Glorify: To accentuate God's honor and dignity; To make God's good name or character known in all that you do.

16. Record some specific attributes (who God is in name and character), provisions (personal ways God has provided) and prayers answered that you are grateful for in your relationship with God. Be sure to thank God!

17. Christian Author C. S. Lewis wrote, "The Psalmists, in telling everyone to praise God, are doing what all men do when they speak of what they care about." If something is important to you, you make it known by talking about it. We declare God's worth and honor by thanking and praising Him. For an example, look up one of the following: *Psalm 48:1-3; 135:1-7; 136; 150.* Write a short psalm that tells God how thankful and grateful you are for Him.

DAILY CONNECTION:

Day 1

In Dr. Timothy Keller's Galatians study, he references three steps that have to occur in order to dismantle idols in your life. (*Galatians Study*, Week 16, "Dismantling Your Idols," Dr. Timothy Keller)

1. Name the Idols
2. Repent of Idols
3. Rejoice: Replacing the Idols

Today, focus on the naming and repenting of idols in your life. Return to Q.9 in this study. Review the list. Take time to journal, reflect on, discuss with others–whatever would help you to name idols in your life. If you are feeling stuck, consider these questions:

What is my greatest fear in sport and life? What brings the most anxiety and worry before, during and after competition? What arouses or incites me to peak performance? What do I rely on, or comfort myself with when things go bad or get difficult? What kinds of thoughts are most repeated in my self-talk during a game? What desires or wishes, if unanswered, would make me neglect or turn from God? Where do I derive my worth and value? What am I proudest of? What do I really want and expect out of life? What delivers the most happiness to me?

After you have formulated your list, take some time and pray that God would put these idols back into the proper place of significance in your life. Ask for forgiveness for making these things more important than God at times. Pray that God would resume his role as Lord of your life so that you enjoy your relationship with God in sport, school, coaching, etc.

Day 2

Idols can oftentimes cause us to inflict pain and harm on ourselves in an effort to gain fulfillment and worth from God-substitutes. The prophets of Baal slashed themselves with swords and spears in an attempt to prove Baal's existence (v. 28) and to get their idol to meet their deepest needs. While keeping the prophets in mind, read the following quotes from Ken Caminiti, an MLB player who died of a drug overdose, that appeared in a *Sports Illustrated* (June 3, 2002) article depicting the use of steroids in Major League Baseball:[8]

"The greatest degree of competition is not for me to compete against you or you against me, but for each of us to reach within the depths of our capabilities and to perform to the greatest of our potential."[7]
(Billy Mills, 1964 Olympic 10,000-meter Gold Medalist)

"I got really strong, really quick," he says. "I pulled a lot of muscles. I broke down a lot. I'm still paying for it. My tendons and ligaments got all torn up. My muscles got too strong for my tendons and ligaments."

Due to steroids, in 1998 alone Caminiti suffered a strained hamstring, a strained quad, a strained calf muscle and a ruptured tendon sheath in his wrist.

Caminiti is now legally prescribed weekly shots of testosterone because of his body's continuing inability to make the hormone in sufficient quantity. "My body's not producing testosterone," he says. "You know what that's like? You get lethargic. You get depressed. It's terrible."

Yet in spite of all these maladies, Caminiti defended his use of steroids and said he would not discourage others from taking them because they have become a widely accepted–even necessary–choice for ballplayers looking for a competitive edge and financial security. "I've made a ton of mistakes," said Caminiti. "I don't think using steroids is one of them."

"You can discover more about a person in an hour of play than in a year of conversation."
(Plato)

"If a young player were to ask me what to do," Caminiti continued, "I'm not going to tell him it's bad. Look at all the money in the game: You have a chance to set your family up, to get your daughter into a better school… So I can't say, 'Don't do it,' not when the guy next to you is as big as a house and he's going to take your job and make the money."

Reflect on the following questions:

1. What idols in Caminiti's life are causing him to harm his body?
2. Idols are oftentimes good things that have been perverted by people trying to make them objects of worship in place of God. What are the righteous aspects of the idols in Caminiti's life? How has he perverted those things?
3. Think back to the list of idols that you made yesterday. How have you harmed yourself in the process of pursuing these idols (emotionally, physically, relationally, etc.)?
4. What good and true aspects of God's creation are behind your idols? How have you over-emphasized the importance of these idols in your life?

Day 3

When something becomes an idol in our lives, it changes the way we view it. We take something around us and exalt it to a place of prominence it shouldn't hold. The displacement causes a skewed view of the object of our idolatry. We begin to place our hopes, aspirations—even identities—on these idols and look to them for fulfillment. More and more of our lives are gradually consumed by these idols in an attempt to elicit the emotional contentment and character validation we all need. In order to succeed in our idolatry, we begin to act in ways that are selfish, deceitful, and sinful. The **Josephson Institute of Ethics** (www.charactercounts.org/sports/survey2004/) conducted a survey in 2004 to find out how high school athletes and coaches think about sport. Let's highlight a few of their findings and contemplate what they say about the role of sports in our lives.

-51% of male athletes and 30% of female athletes endorse their coaches arguing with an official to intimidate or influence future calls.

-45% of male athletes and 22% of female athletes think a coach should teach a player how to cheat without being caught.

-27% of females and 43% of males believe that to succeed in sport a person has to lie or cheat sometimes.

1. Do you agree with the beliefs of these high school athletes? Why or why not?

2. Do these statements represent an (**Audience of One**) perspective? Why or why not?

3. How would a God-glorifying view of sport change these perspectives?

4. What are beliefs you hold about your own sport that need reform?

Day 4

Now that we are starting to understand how idols can influence the way we compete, let's practice our ability to pick these themes out by observing a group of athletes in the midst of their competition. Watch the movie *Friday Night Lights.* While watching, try to identify the various idols in the athletes' lives. Then think through and discuss the effects of these idols. In particular, observe the characters of James "Boobie" Miles and Don Billingsly. Why are they competing? Who are they playing for? What are the consequences of their idolatry? Would their actions/responses look any different if they understood and embodied the (**Audience of One**) principle? How? Be specific.

Day 5

We have the opportunity to rejoice and set our mind on Christ instead of on our idols. Dr. Timothy Keller states, "What you rejoice in is the thing that is your central sweetness and consolation in life. To rejoice is to treasure a thing, to assess its value to you, to reflect on its beauty and importance until your heart rests in it and tastes the sweetness of it.

Rejoicing is a way of praising God until the heart is sweetened and rested, and until it relaxes its grip on anything else it thinks it needs." (*Galatians Study*, Dr. Timothy Keller)

Use the following prayer from *31 Days of Praise*, by Ruth Meyers, to rejoice in who God is:

My heart rejoices in you, Lord, for you are my strong shelter in times of trouble and danger and stress, my hiding place to whom I may continually resort, my Father who lovingly provides for me, my Shepherd who guides and protects me, my Champion who upholds my cause as His child and defends my highest interests, my bridegroom who delights in me, my God who is mighty to save, who rests in His love for me and rejoices over me with singing, with shouts of joy. You are my inheritance, my share in life, the One who satisfies my longing soul and fills my hungry soul with goodness. [9]

Try going for a walk, praying this as you walk. Or tape this to your locker and lift it up to God each day before practice and games. Find time daily to reflect on the truth of who God is and what He has done in your life.

REMINDERS:

1. Because God is our ultimate Audience, Lord of your sport and life, everything is to be done for His glory.

2. Sport is a good pursuit but, like any other activity, it is susceptible to perversion by being made all important, the center of your life—defining you and giving you ultimate meaning in life—an idol.

3. It is not by any accident that you were created in God's image with unique talents and gifts that can be creatively and worthily expressed through sport for worship.

4. Worship through sport is an expression of your appreciation and gratitude to God with your whole being (**Thank-You Response**), as you humbly compete with respect for the game, the rules, the coaches, the athletes, the fans, your body, the officials, and the team.

5. We do not compete or perform for God, for this would imply that we must do something to earn his favor or acceptance.

"...praise (God) with your wholeselves: that is, let not your tongue and voice alone praise God, but your conscience also, your life, your deeds."

(St. Augustine, 5th Century Bishop of North Africa)

NOTES:

1. Harry Edwards, *Sociology of Sport* (Homewood, IL.: Dorsey Press, 1973), 261-62.

2. Os Guinness and John Seel, *No God But God: Breaking with the Idols of Our Age* (Chicago, IL.: Moody Press, 1992).

3. J. Richard Middleton and Brain J. Walsh, *The Transforming Vision* (Downers Grove, IL.: InterVarsity Press, 1984), 62.

4. Tim Keller, *SOSL Year 1 Participant's Guide 4.1* (adapted and contextualized); For up-to-date resources, see www.redeemer2.com/resources; www.godsquad.com/squadroom/ discipleship/Galatians.

5. John Paul II, "Address to the International Olympic Committee about the value of sports" on 27 May 1982.

6. Greg Johnson, *The World According to God: A Biblical View of Culture, Work, Science, Sex and Everything Else* (Downers Grove, IL: InterVarsity Press, 2002), 24-25.

7. Lorne A. Adrian, *The Most Important Thing I Know about the Spirit of Sport: 101 Inspiring Messages from Athletes, Coaches, Sportswriters, and Commentators* (New York: William Morrow and Co., 1999), 114.

8. Tom Verduci, "Caminiti Comes Clean," *Sports Illustrated* (28 May 2002) Online; available from http://sportsillustrated.cnn.com/si_online/special_report/steroids/ [accessed 23 February 2006].

9. Ruth Myers, *31 Days of Praise* (Sisters, OR.: Multnomah, 2002), 40.

RESOURCES:

Bruce Ellis Benson, *Graven Ideologies: Nietzche, Derrida & Marion on Modern Idolatry.*

Elyse Fitzpatrick, *Idols of the Heart: Learning to Long for God Alone.*

Os Guinness and John Seel, *No God But God: Breaking with the Idols of Our Age.*

Tim Keller, *SOSL Year 1 Participant's Guide 4.1.*

Paul Marshall, *Heaven is Not My Home.*

J. Richard Middleton and Brain J. Walsh, *The Transforming Vision.*

Ruth Myers, *31 Days of Praise.*

Edward Welch, "Motives: Why Do I Do the Things I Do?" in *The Journal of Biblical Counseling* Fall 2003.

Michael Wittmer, *Heaven is a Place on Earth: Why Everything You Do Matters To God.*

ENGAGING CULTURE RESOURCES:

John Barber, *Earth Restored.*

William Dyrness, *Visual Faith: Art, Theology, and Worship in Dialogue.*

John R. Gerdy, *Sports: The All-American Addiction.*

Greg Johnson, *The World According to God.*

T.M. Moore, *Redeeming Pop Culture.*

Cornelius Plantinga, *Engaging God's World: A Christian Vision of Faith, Learning and Living.*

William Romanowski, *Eyes Wide Open: Looking for God in Pop Culture.*

"I'm thankful to know that whether I experience failure or success, God always has my back. Furthermore, my win/loss record has zero bearing on my status with Him. God loves me for who I am, not what I do. And He loves you just the same." (Lorenzo Romar, NCAA Head Basketball Coach)

Concentrate! Focus! Get psyched! Easy! Whether your coach reminds you or your inner-coach whispers to you, we all know that in order to reach your peak performance something has to be done with what is going on in the inside—that mind game, soul stuff and heart matter.

The Christian story speaks to your soul about the necessary, interior, heart change made possible by God's love and grace; this change is what enables you to live and compete with God as your Audience. Because of Christ, God's love and grace are now "intrinsic" to you by faith as His adopted child. That means your new, intrinsic motivation in Christ frees you to mentally and emotionally cope with factors like fear, anxiety, anger, pressure, guilt, worry, self-doubt, and negative self-talk, which can prevent and disrupt you from flourishing as a human being and experiencing in sport that optimal experience called "flow" or "in the zone." God's love releases you to enjoy and completely go for it without feeling trapped by your fear of failure or rejection associated with your performance, the outcome of the contest.

P|2
C|2

2 Chapter

PRINCIPLE TWO

Luke 15:11-32 "The Story of the Prodigal Son"

Inside Game

GOD'S LOVE IS THE MAXIMUM MOTIVATION

Our identity in Christ frees us to compete with a "grace motivation."

Inside Game

CONTEMPORARY CONNECTION:

In sports, I am most motivated to play intensely when...

____ I don't make any mistakes.
____ The coaches tell me I did a good job.
____ The media recognizes my performance.
____ I beat my toughest opponent.
____ My parents are very proud of me as an athlete.
____ I push myself to the limits.
____ I am competing against our number one rival.
____ There are a lot of fans and spectators watching me.
____ We might make it to the championship.
____ I work harder than everyone else.
____ I am competing against a team that often beats me.
____ I am enjoying and loving the game.
____ The rewards (money and medals) are great.
____ The camaraderie and team spirit is strong.
____ I am developing and refining my skills.

"The first thing is to love your sport. Never do it to please someone else. It has to be yours."

(Peggy Fleming, 1968 Olympic Figure Skating Gold Medalist)

> "It isn't the money. It's the hunger, the desire, and it's hard to turn it off. It's about pride, and it's about ego."
> (Chris Evert, former Professional Women's Tennis Player)

Definition of motivation:

The reason or desire a person adopts for doing something or participating in a particular activity. Why you do what you do. Sport psychologists typically designate two kinds of motivation: *intrinsic* and *extrinsic*. *Intrinsic motivation* is doing sport simply for the sheer pleasure and satisfaction derived from the competition itself (i.e., enjoy playing, excitement, skill development, teamwork, etc.) or within the sport experience. *Extrinsic motivation* is sport behavior based on something that is the result or product of competition (i.e., awards, money, fame, winning, recognition, acceptance, etc.), and thus, sport is a means to some other external end or outcome.

Further reflection:
Which kind of motivation typifies your competition?

HISTORICAL CONNECTION:

The Pharisees were a movement of Jewish, devoutly religious leaders who sought a strict adherence to the Law (Old Testament) as interpreted by the scribes. The Gospels depict the Pharisees as critical and hostile toward Jesus. Instead of defending His actions, Jesus tells a story of two sons that exposes and corrects the true motivations of the leaders who criticized him.

⇣Further study: Look up Pharisee in a Bible dictionary. Cross reference these verses: Matt. 23:23-28 Luke 18:9-14 Matt. 6:1-5

In the first century A.D., Jewish law required that a father divide everything he owned between his sons. The law specified that the eldest son receive two-thirds of the inheritance and that the younger son receive one-third. Since this would typically happen near the end of a father's life, the younger son in this story insults his father and rejects his duties as a son when he asks for his inheritance early. The emotional shock of this son's request would have been extreme.[1]

Jesus would often use parables—stories of common things that mirror spiritual truths. Read *Luke 15:11-32*. In Luke 15, Jesus is criticized by the religious leaders (Pharisees) for accepting despised people (tax collectors and sinners) (see *Luke 5:29-31*).

BIBLICAL CONNECTION:

Read *Luke 15:11-32.*

⇣Further reflection: The people listening to Jesus' parables would have immediately identified with the points of the story. His audience would have been shocked by the turn of events in the story as Jesus was providing them with a new understanding of God's kingdom. What points of the story may (speculate) have been shocking to this Jewish audience as the story unfolded ?

1. How do you initially respond to the three main characters in this story? Do you agree with their actions? Why or why not?

2. With the Pharisees' criticism in mind, what do you think is the main idea of this story?

Record the answers to the following questions in the chart on page 67.

3. Record, in order, a list (in your own words) of the younger son's actions once he left home. The emotions of the story are deep and wide-ranging.

In the same chart, record the younger son's feelings (v. 12, 16-19, 21).

Further reflection:
Inside View: The turning point literally and spiritually for the younger son is observed in verses 17-19 when "he came to his senses". Count the number of first-person (internal dialogue-"I" statements) comments the son makes about his situation in these few verses. What does this say about the younger son's understanding of his actions and lifestyle? Why is this personal assessment or evaluation needed before returning home?

Definition of inheritance:
The Greek word for inheritance is *ton bion* which literally means "the life". The son is requesting his portion of what his father's life will leave him.[2]

4. Record, on your chart, his motivations and the result of his search. What was he seeking? Did he find "the life" he was looking for?

HISTORICAL CONNECTION:
The younger son sinks to an all-time low. As a Jewish son, to join himself to Gentiles (v. 15) and to be associated with pigs was both thoroughly disgusting and religiously offensive and unclean. It would have been equivalent to renouncing your religion because you would not have been permitted to worship while in these circumstances.

Further application:
Have you ever admitted (confessed) your need for God to this degree? How is this son's experience similar to 1 John 1:9 and Psalm 51:1-4? Take some time to personally and honestly admit your struggles, waywardness, and distance from God like the younger son did.

The younger son believes that a life of independence and freedom, the ability to do whatever he wants, will bring him ultimate happiness. He soon realizes, however, that what he initially sought was temporary and would not deeply satisfy him. This realization is witnessed in the story by this inward turn (v. 17-19)–a repentant spirit.

Can you think of a situation when something was so important that you pursued it doggedly, only to have it turn out completely different than you had hoped or expected? Describe how you felt.

5. What emotions and actions characterize the older son's response to the younger son's return? (See v. 26-30) (Record in the chart on page 67) How varied and different are the two sons' emotions?

"We never had enough to eat, and I became angry, and my anger stayed with me through my career. It drove me."[3]
(Isaiah Thomas, former NBA Player)

6. (Record in the same chart) What motivated him in his relationship with his father? What effect/result did this have in his relationship with his father and brother? Why couldn't the older son celebrate with his brother? (See v. 25-30)

> "I feel I'm the best player out there and no one can stop me. I want to beat you and embarrass you bad. But I don't want people to know that. It's like a little secret I keep to myself."[4]
> (Grant Hill, NBA Player)

The older son believed that he could earn his father's love through obedience and hard work. Instead of enjoying his father's love, however, he reacted with bitterness when he saw that his father also loved the son who had not worked for his love.

7. Can you relate to his feelings? Why or why not?

8. How would the Pharisees who were listening have felt if the story had ended in verse 24?

What was Jesus trying to teach them through the character of the older son?

9. In what situations, do you most identify with the younger son and/or the older son? Why?

10. Using the chart on page 67, list the father's actions, emotions, motivation and result as he relates to each of his sons (younger son: v. 12, 20, 22, 23, 24; older son: v. 28, 31, 32). What characteristics of God does the father exemplify?

Further reflection: How have your parents (especially your father) positively and negatively affected your involvement and motivation in sport? What affect might an absent parent, missing father, or pushy parent have on a sportsperson's outlook? How does the father in this story go beyond your own parent's successes and failures?

"He [Wayne Gretzky] could be very motivated by things in newspaper articles, what people said about him. If somebody said something about him being a whiner, he really got ticked. It was purely a pride thing."[5]
(Glen Sather, Coach of Edmonton Oilers)

11. How was the father's perspective of the two sons different than how the sons thought he viewed them? Contrast the differing perceptions.

Sport Factoids:

1. Parents are the main socializers influencing children's sport involvement. Fathers have typically been found to be the most important socialization influence for both boys and girls.[6]
2. More than 75 % of grown-ups polled in Florida agreed that parents involved in youth sports are too aggressive.[7]

HISTORICAL CONNECTION:

Jesus' audience would have quickly recognized that the father's pursuit (he saw, ran, embraced and kissed his son) indicated full-restoration by the following points of the story: 1) the robe-this was the father's actual robe, 2) the ring-this was the family's signet ring signifying the son's reinstated position (versus a hired laborer), 3) the sandals-these symbolized that the son was free indeed for slaves do not typically wear sandals, 4) the calf-this signified that this was a major block party with dancing and all.

"My dad never pushed me but the big thing is that he helped me by going out in the backyard and playing with me."

(Bart Starr, former NFL Quarterback)

12. Freedom is experienced by understanding God the Father's love and grace toward you as was exhibited in the Prodigal Son story.

> Both sons wanted the wealth of the father without the father. The younger son was crying for freedom and looking out. The older son was crying for freedom and looking in. The father wants to provide freedom by looking to Him.

Correct: Your relationship with God defines your self-worth:
Self-worth = what God declares is true about you.

Incorrect: We have a poor formula for self worth:
Self-worth=Our performance + Others' opinions.

Look up the following verses. List what God's love has accomplished in order to set you free forever (see a more complete list at the end of chapter 2).

P|2
C|2

1 John 4:9-10:

2 Cor. 5:17-21:

Col. 1:19-22:

Rom. 8:1:

Rom. 8:35-39:

"Today, I am more confident in my game than ever because I know God loves me regardless of how I perform."
(Ruth Riley, WNBA Player)

SPORT CONNECTION:

"So as young sports stars grow older, their reputation as a winner gradually becomes the only joy sport still offers them. At first, the rewards of winning seem worth the cost. Adolescence is all about peer acceptance, and there is no more certain way to gain the approval and admiration of other Americans than by being a star athlete. Eventually, however, even the joy that comes from being a star begins to fade.

Since being special in sport is the only thing such athletes have going for them, winning becomes the focus of their life. If they don't perform well, they punish themselves emotionally. They tell themselves how no good they are for letting themselves "mess up" and become a loser. They learn to rely on this self-hatred to force themselves to train harder and longer until they become a winner again.

Unfortunately, even winning is not much better for their emotional health. The thrill of victory is short-lived. To keep feeling that joy, sports stars must win over and over again. Like an addict who needs even higher doses of his drug to enjoy the same high, it is not enough to just win at the same level as before." [9]

"An athlete cannot run with money in his pockets. He must run with hope in his heart and dreams in his head."

(Emil Zatopek, 1952 Olympic 5,000, 10,000-meter and the Marathon Gold Medalist from the Czech Republic)

Reflect:

To what extent is the above passage true for people in sport today? Can you relate to this challenge and pressure?

"Three lies of false masculinity: Athletic ability, sexual conquest and economic success." [8]

(Joe Ehrmann, former NFL Player)

Harold Abrahams, one of the top British sprinters in the 1924 Olympics, like others ran to prove his worth. Right before one of his big races, he confided in his teammate (as depicted in the movie, *Chariots of Fire*):

"I'm twenty-four—and I've never known contentment. I'm forever in pursuit—and I don't even know what it is I am chasing. I'm scared... In one hour's time, I'll be out there again. I'll raise my eyes and look down that corridor – four feet wide with ten lonely seconds to justify my whole existence. But will I!" [10]

Harold Abrahams perceived that his value as a human being was largely based on his success as an athlete. *Good athletes are highly motivated but often for the wrong reasons.*

13. **Group exercise:** Let's suppose you are having one of those days: a sorry practice, two days ago you missed the game-winning shot, and you said and did some things that are less than becoming of who you are as a Christ-follower. To say the least, your feelings and motivations have been up and down as you work-out much like the two sons from our story.

If you were to make the necessary adjustments to your (**Inside Game**) (internally in what you believe about yourself in relation to God's love and grace), what truths from the list on page 68 would you need to "lock-on" or "hold on" to in order to combat that negative self-talk and the accompanying poor motivations for why you even compete? In other words, based on the Father's love and grace (Q.12 & see complete list on page 68), verbally share 1-2 things from this study that are true of you regardless of whether circumstances are going well. Write these down.

14. How might God's truth about you (Q.12 & see complete list) free you to compete without worrying about either your performance or the opinions of your coaches, teammates, athletic director, fans, peers, administrators, etc.? Give an example and be specific about what this could look like.

"To succeed... you need to find something to hold on to, something to motivate you, something to inspire you."
(Tony Dorsett, former NFL Player)

Further reflection: Go to the following web site and view the painting by Rembrandt illustrating this Bible passage, **The Return of the Prodigal** Son: (http://www.Hermitagemuseum.org/html_En/03/hm3_3_1_4d.html) Describe what you see and feel. How does this help you connect with God's fatherly love and compassion?

Putting It Together: JUST BE IT

"Competitive sports are played mainly on a five-and-a-half inch court, the space between your ears."
(Bobby Jones, former Pro Golfer)

In sport, there are plenty of good and healthy motivations, but the challenge is to clock-on" to the ultimate motivation (**based on Christ's love and grace**) regardless of outside circumstances: the score is in your favor, your coach is pleased with you, your contract is up for renewal, the fans are accepting of you, you are playing in the zone, etc. On account of Christ, you now have an intrinsic motivation that never changes or fluctuates due to circumstances. His love and grace are 100% reliable (constant) and never subject to your performance. Begin meditating on and believing (see page 68) what is true of you so that you can personally experience God's motivation in your competition and life. It will be manifested in how you compete: constant intensity, positive self-talk, attitude adjustments, control of emotions, maintaining appropriate focus, confidence, feeling good about yourself and a proper evaluation of performance, right motivation to perform, etc.

"True gratitude or thankfulness to God for his kindness to us, arises from a foundation laid before, of love to God for what he is in himself..."[11]
(Jonathan Edwards, 18th Century Theologian and Pastor)

GOD CONNECTION:

15. What has God taught you about yourself and your motivations for competition?

16. What is it about God's love and grace that you need to apply to your life today? Be specific with respect to your own struggles and drama this week/year in your life.

17. Read and memorize *2 Cor. 5:14-15.* Write a prayer of gratitude for what God has done. (**Thank-You Response**) Allow this to be what you thank God for as you pass, block, obey the rules, run an extra sprint, and respect the game, etc.

DAILY CONNECTION:

Day 1

We must always be striving to synthesize what God is teaching us intellectually through scripture with how we live on a daily basis. In our first two daily connections, let's focus on how the principles in this chapter can affect the way we compete in our sport.

Study the list on (page 68). Choose a couple of the statements that excite you the most and write them on an index card. Pray through each truth, thinking deeply about how it changes the way you view yourself (**Inside Game**). Thank God for the freedom that comes with His love and the assurance that you will never be unworthy to Him based on your performance.

Tape the index card up in your locker or to the dash in your car—somewhere that you will see it every day on your way to compete. Before each athletic endeavor, repeat praying through each truth and thanking God for your freedom. This is who you are.

"In the field of sports you are more or less accepted for what you do rather than what you are."

(Althea Gibson, first African-American to compete at Wimbledon)

Day 2

After reflecting on God's truths for your life (**Daily Connection Day 1**), go out and worship Him through your athletic gifts by rejoicing in His freedom while you compete. Know that what God declares is true about you will not change according to how well you play. Use this as encouragement to work even harder and play with even more passion out of joyful gratitude for God's gracious and unconditional love in your life. Whenever you have a break in the action–between plays, in a timeout, in-between reps, etc., pray and thank Christ for His role in your life, continually dedicating your performance to Him.

Afterwards, think through and process how well you were able to do this. Did you really feel motivated by God's love, or did you revert back to your old motivations in the midst of competition? What were your emotions while playing? How was your intensity?

Don't be discouraged if you have trouble mastering this principle the first time out.

You have been programmed to compete a certain way your entire life and it will require time and effort to rewire the way you think. Just continue to repeat this process every time you have the opportunity to use the athletic abilities God has blessed you with—whether in the weight room, on the practice field, or in a game. As with many spiritual disciplines, it will take energy and intent, but eventually you will see fruit.

"Preach the Gospel at all times. If necessary, use words."
(St. Francis of Assisi)

> "Football [sports] is a profession that is judged by performance and results. However, those things come and go so quickly that, as a coach, I have to base my career on something more. Don't get me wrong: I want the Colts to win, but if that were all we did, it would be pretty shallow. I want to win, but I want to do it with the right type of guys, role models for the children and families of Indianapolis. I want to help mold a team that the entire city can be proud of."
> (Tony Dungy, NFL Coach)

Day 3

"Do you know what my favorite part of the game is? The opportunity to play."
(Mike Singletary, former NFL Player)

Read the following quotes from prominent athletic figures about success in their sport. While reading, think about what motivation to compete is reflected in each statement.

"My victory has proved that athletes with yellow skin can run as fast as those with black and white skin." (winning the men's 110 meters hurdles in a world record-equaling time of 12.91 seconds)
Liu Xiang

"I don't think there's anything more painful in the world." (the honest, exclamation from a tearful U.S. wrestler who lost to Kaori Icho of Japan in the last minute of their gold medal bout in the 63 kg category)
Sara McMann

"The will to win is worthless if you don't get paid for it."
Reggie Jackson

"Winning isn't everything, it's the only thing."
Vince Lombardi

"I hated every minute of training, but I said, Don't quit. Suffer now and live the rest of your life as a champion."
Muhammad Ali

"Whoever said, 'It's not whether you win or lose that counts,' probably lost."
Martina Navratilova

Answer the following questions:

a. Look at each quote individually. What is motivating these people to succeed?

b. Which of these motivations is most present in your life? How does it drive you?

c. What were the initial motivations and results of the two brothers in the Parable of the Prodigal Son? How might the motivations of the athletes above lead to a similar demise?

d. How have certain motivations led to disappointment and a lack of self-worth in your past?

e. Why are motivations outside of God bound to eventually lead to a sense of failure?

> "One thing that God has taught me through football is to try and phase out the circumstances around me and not let them control me."
> (Frank Reich, former NFL Quarterback, known for leading the greatest comeback in NFL history in the 1992 playoffs.)

> True Story:
> After Bobby Jones called the penalty stroke on himself, he was praised by the officials for his honesty. He retorted, "You might as well praise me for not breaking into banks. There is only one way to play this game."[12]
> (Craig Lambert, *Harvard Magazine*)

Day 4

At times, we cannot truly understand our motivations for competing until we step back and analyze our actions in the midst of competition. In the final round of the 1925 U.S. Open, Bobby Jones was deadlocked with his rival Walter Hagen. Towards the end of their round, Jones got ready to hit an approach shot onto the green. While addressing his ball, Jones accidentally nudged it, causing it to move so slightly it was undetectable to any eye but his. He immediately called a penalty on himself, costing him a stroke. The officials and his opponent conferred and all encouraged Jones not to take the penalty because no one but him had seen the ball move. Jones, however, knew that he had in fact caused the motion and took the required penalty. Jones lost the Open Championship to Hagen by one stroke.

a. What do Jones' actions say about his motivations in competition?

b. Why is it important to play honorably and by the rules?

c. How would Jones' actions been different had he been motivated by a utilitarian, 'win-at-all-costs' mentality?

d. Think of a situation in your sport when you may have overlooked, ignored, or intentionally broken a rule in order to succeed. What should you have done and why?

Day 5

So far, we have looked at what drives us to play our sport. We have been studying our motivations, similarly to how we studied the motivations of the two brothers in the Parable of the Prodigal Son. Now, let's focus on the unconditional love of the father and our call to love others in that same way. What does this have to do with our lives as athletes?

We are surrounded by teammates and coaches daily. We may spend more time with these people than anyone else at this point in our lives. These are people with whom we can share the unconditional love of our heavenly Father, just as the father in our passage shared his love with his sons.

Think of a few of your teammates or coaches who could use some encouragement. Think of specific ways in which you can love them. It can be anything from a kind word of affirmation, an act of service, a gift, consistent prayer for that person, time spent hanging out with them, etc. You never know how God can use a seemingly small act of love in a person's life to encourage them.

There is no better witness we can have for the gospel than by loving people with grace–this means loving them even when (or maybe especially when) they don't deserve it. That is how the Father loves us!

> "Of course, even after I became a Christian, I still felt the pressure. The grind of an 82-game schedule, expectations from fans, constant scrutiny from the media, and the challenge of giving leadership to my team were all very demanding... But with all of these pressures, I had to lean hard on God to help me keep an even keel... I don't have to trust in what I can do. I just need to trust in what God can do through me."
> (David Robinson, Two-time NBA Champion and Olympic Gold Medalist)

REMINDERS:

1. In Christ, the quest to prove, to achieve, or to validate your worth as an athlete or coach is satisfied. You are completely accepted and loved by God.

2. You are motivated by God's love to freely compete and live without being overly anxious about, worrying about, or fearing *your performance* (e.g. wins, losses, starting position, etc.).

3. You are motivated by God's love to freely compete and live without being overly anxious about, worrying about, or fearing the *opinions of others* (e.g. peers, coaches, teammates, athletic director, fans, administrators, etc.).

4. God's Word, the Bible, includes innumerable truths about you as God's child which will remind you of His love and help you cope with the frustrations, fears, mistakes, and pressures in the ups and downs of sport and life.

5. Like the prodigal son, when you make a mistake or fail in sport and life, God, the Father, is running to meet you and take you in His arms and hold you close for He loves and forgives you unconditionally.

NOTES:

1. Craig Keener, *The IVP Bible Background Commentary* (Downers Grove, IL.: InterVarsity Press, 1993), 232-33.

2. Darrell Bock, *Luke Baker Exegetical Commentary on the New Testament* Vol.2 (Grand Rapids, MI.: Baker Books, 1996), 1309.

3. Michael Clarkson, *Competitive Drive* (Champaign, IL.: Human Kinetics, 1999), 85.

4. Christopher John Farley, "Gentleman Slam Dunker," *Time* 145, no. 6 (13 February 1995), 78.

5. Clarkson, *Competitive Drive*, 82.

6. S.L. Greendorfer, J.H. Lewko, and K.S. Rosengren, "Family influence in sport socialization: Sociocultural Perspectives," in F. Smoll and R. Smith (Eds.), *Children and youth in sport* (Dubuque, IA: Brown and Benchmark, 1996), 89-111; http://ed- web3.educ.msu.edu./ysi/project/ CriticalIssuesYouthSports.pdf. (Institute for the Study of Youth Sports); *See also* R. Brustad, M. Babkes, and A. Smith. "Youth in sport: Psychological considerations," in R. Singer, H. Hausenblas, and C. Janelle (Eds.), *Handbook of Sport Psychology* (New York: Wiley, 2001), 604-635.

7. Rachel S. Cox, "Sportsmanship," *The CQ Researcher* 11, no.11, (23 March 2001), 229.

8. Jeffrey Marx, *Season of Life* (New York: Simon & Schuster, 2003), 70-73.

9. John Ashley Null, *Real Joy: Freedom to be Your Best* (Germany: Ebner & Spiegel, Ulm, 2004), 11.

10. *Ibid.*, 161.

11. Jonathan Edwards, "Religious Affections," *The Works of Jonathan Edwards,* Vol. 2, (New Haven: Yale University Press, 1959, orig. 1746), 247.

12. Craig Lambert, "Bobby Jones" (March-April 2002) Online; available from http://www.harvardmagazine.com/on-line/030220.html [accessed 10 September 2005].

RESOURCES:

Darrell Bock, *Luke: Baker Exegetical Commentary on the New Testament.*

Arthur P. Ciaramicoli, *The Performance Addiction.*

Jeffrey Marx, *Season of Life: A Football Star, a Boy, a Journey to Manhood.*

Robert S. McGee, *Search for Significance.*

Henri Nouwen, *The Return of the Prodigal Son.*

John Ashley Null, *Real Joy: Freedom to be Your Best.*

Jim Taylor and Gregory Wilson, (ed.), *Applying Sport Psychology.*

Robin S. Vealey, *Coaching for the Inner Edge.*

Robert S. Weinberg and Daniel Gould, *Foundations of Sport and Exercise Psychology.*

	Action	Emotion	Motivation	Result
Younger Son				
Older Son				
Father				

SELF-WORTH: GOD'S TRUTH ABOUT YOU

1. I am **accepted** and **worthy**. *Romans 15:7; Psalm 139*
2. I am **never alone**. *Hebrews 13:5b; Romans 8:38, 39*
3. I am **adequate**. *II Corinthians 3:5,6; Philippians 4:13*
4. I have **boldness** and **confidence**. *Proverbs 3:26; 14:26; Hebrews 10:19*
5. God will be **faithful** to me. *Philippians 1:6; 2:13; II Thessalonians 3:3*
6. I have the **mind of Christ**. *I Corinthians 2:16; Philippians 2:5*
7. I have **hope**. *Romans 15:13; Psalm 33:17-18*
8. I am seen as **perfect**. *Hebrews 10:14; Colossians 2:13*
9. I have been **chosen** and **set apart**. *Ephesians 1:4*
10. I **lack nothing**. *Philippians 4:19*
11. I am **free from fear**. *Psalm 34:4; II Timothy 1:7*
12. I have all the **faith** I need. *Romans 12:3*
13. I have **strength**. *Daniel 11:32; Psalm 37:39*
14. I am **victorious**. *Romans 8:37; II Corinthians 2:14*
15. I have **wisdom**. *Proverbs 2:6, 7; I Corinthians 1:30*
16. I am **free**. *Psalm 32:7; II Corinthians 3:17*
17. I have **comfort**. *II Corinthians 1:3,4*
18. I am **protected**. *Psalm 32:7*
19. I am **perfectly loved**. *John 15:9; Romans 8:38, 39; Ephesians 2:4, 5; 5:1*
20. I am an **adopted child of God**. *Romans 8:16; Galatians 4:5; Ephesians 1:5*
21. I am **totally forgiven**. *Psalm 103:12; John 1:29; Ephesians 1:7*
22. I have been **declared righteous**. *Romans 3:24; I Corinthians 1:30; 6:11*
23. I am **indwelt by the Holy Spirit**. *Acts 1:8; I Corinthians 12:13; II Timothy 1:14*
24. I have **direct access** to God. *Romans 5:1-2; Ephesians 2:18; 3:12*
25. I am **blameless**. *John 3:18; Romans 8:1*
26. I have been **created for good works**. *Ephesians 2:10; II Timothy 2:21; 3:16-17*
27. I am a **new creation**. *II Corinthians 5:17*
28. I have **authority** over Satan. *Colossians 1:13; I John 4:4*
29. I am **dead to sin**. *Romans 6:11*
30. I am **dead to the law**. *Romans 6:14; 7:4-6*
31. I have an **eternal inheritance**. *Romans 8:16-17; Ephesians 1:11,14,18*
32. I have been **raised with Christ**. *Romans 6:4-8; Galatians 2:20; Colossians 2:12*
33. I will be **with Christ in heaven**. *Philippians 3:20-21; Revelation 21-22*
34. I have **eternal security**. *I John 5:11-13; John 10:27-30*
35. I have **spiritual gifts** for His service. *I Corinthians 12*

"Sports do not build character. They reveal it."
(John Wooden, former NCAA Basketball Coach)

Does sport build or reveal character? Regardless of your conviction or opinion, sport is a physical activity involving human beings who feel, act and make real choices, a spiritual thing for sure!

In sport, all the competitors strive toward a goal. For an athlete or coach, the striving and desire to win is important. Jesse Owens retorted, "If you don't try to win you might as well hold the Olympics in somebody's back yard." Equally important is the manner in which we seek to achieve that goal of winning. You might say we have a double goal: win with "excellence in competition" and with "excellence in character". These are not mutually exclusive!

Authentic Christianity is marked by the excellent character and conduct of Christ. We have been called to be "little Christs" in our very attitudes, dispositions and actions. Your goal is to mature and become like Jesus Christ. This is a holy calling that involves a spiritual workout of sorts—sweat and all.

God shapes our character and spiritual formation in Christian community through a cooperative relationship between us and His Spirit. His Spirit fills and empowers us by providing such resources as: the Bible for studying and meditating, prayer for transparent conversation, and solitude for silencing all the other voices of ordinary life — all to cultivate His character in sport and life, and all before an (**Audience of One**).

3

PRINCIPLE THREE Chapter

Luke 4:1-13 "The Temptation of Jesus"

Holy Sweat

GOD PROVIDES RESOURCES FOR SPIRITUAL TRAINING TO CULTIVATE CHRISTLIKE CHARACTER

Maturity is a process of God's Spirit growing us in grace 'over time' through the spiritual disciplines that cultivate Christlike habits and character traits.

Holy Sweat

CONTEMPORARY CONNECTION:

Who are some of your role models? Why? Can you describe anything about their background, family, sport, or history that helped them earn that role?

Often, what we admire most are those personal character qualities (see Kareem Abdul-Jabbar's quote) that found expression in their excellent accomplishments or achievements.

"All the courage and competitiveness of Jackie Robinson affects me to this day. If I patterned my life after anyone it was him, not because he was the first black baseball player in the majors but because he was a hero."
(Kareem Abdul-Jabbar, former NBA Player)

1. We are not to train only our bodies, but our souls as well. Read the verse below and discuss the purpose and priority for "training our souls".

"Train yourself in godliness, for, while physical training is of some value, godliness is valuable in every way, holding promise for the present life and the life to come." (1 Tim. 4:7-8, NRSV).

2. What are some ways you train physically for your sport? How is this similar and different to soul/spiritual training? What are some ways of training for spiritual fitness?

In sport, we understand the need for physical training in order to improve. Oftentimes, in our spiritual lives, however, we lack the direct correlation between our walk with God and the need to train our souls for godliness. It wasn't by accident that Jesus displayed godliness in all he did. He made his relationship with God his highest priority.

3. What types of exercises are in your spiritual training now?

↓Further study:
Cross-reference: Deut. 8:1-3. List the commands and the purposes for them. This was Jesus' religious heritage and as a young Jewish boy he would have been instructed by his parents according to this very passage.

What obstacles do you face in your circumstances or personal life that make soul-training difficult?

> "If we have faith in Christ, we must believe that he knew how to live. We can, through faith and grace, become like Christ by practicing the types of activities he engaged in, by arranging our whole lives around the activities he himself practiced in order to remain constantly at home in the fellowship of his Father."[1]

HISTORICAL CONNECTION:

Luke 4:1-13 is called the temptation of Jesus and is situated between two important events: God confirming Jesus' sonship and the earthly mission of Jesus. In Luke chapter 3, John the Baptist is preaching about One who is to come, the true Messiah. Once John baptized Jesus, the Holy Spirit descended upon Jesus and God said, "This is My Son, in whom I am well pleased" (*3:22*). This voice from heaven confirmed His identity. But before Jesus would launch out into His public ministry, it was necessary for his resolve to be tested. Therefore, the Holy Spirit led him into the wilderness to be tempted by Satan for 40 days, without food. It is one thing to talk about identity and another to authenticate it. Jesus passed the test and immediately went out to preach and teach (*4:15*). His private battle prepared him for his public ministry. This demonstrated that Jesus' motivation affirmed God as His audience—(**Audience of One.**)

↓Further reflection:
As a coach and/or a parent, how are you instructing your student-athletes and children in the ways of the Lord?

BIBLICAL CONNECTION:

Read *Luke 4:1-13*

4. Who are the main characters in this story and what is the primary purpose of each character?

Geographically, the Judean wilderness is the area north of the Dead Sea and on both sides of the Jordan River valley. It is a hilly area that is semi-desert. Metaphorically, the wilderness here represents a place of solitude and barrenness, where all of one's comforts are stripped away.

5. How does the narrator describe the role/actions and relationship of the Holy Spirit to Jesus in this passage? Why are these details important for us to know as we even think about our own growth and the temptations we will face?

6. The Holy Spirit led Jesus into the *wilderness* for forty days, without food and all alone. Why not into the temple where he could pray, study the Scriptures and eat a healthy diet?

Further study:
What do these verses say about the Holy Spirit? Jn. 16:5-15
Rom. 8:1-17
Gal. 5:16-26
Describe the role of the Spirit in affecting change in our lives.

7. Why did the devil wait until the end of 40 days to tempt Jesus?

↓Further study: Use a Bible dictionary and look up other names for the devil: Satan, the evil one, slanderer, liar, deceiver, accuser, angel of light, prince of this world, tempter, destroyer. Write a brief description.

8. Think through the areas and the circumstances when you are most likely to yield to temptation. Is it in the heat of competition? After much success? Failure? When you are alone?

Below is a chart for the three temptations and Jesus' response to each. Read through each temptation, record what the devil was appealing to and how Jesus responded.

"I believe ability can get you to the top, but it takes character to keep you there. A big part of character is the self-discipline needed to avoid complacency, resist temptation, and understand that past success doesn't guarantee future success."

(John Wooden, former NCAA Basketball Coach)

Verse	The Devil's Temptation	Jesus' Response
4:3-4		
4:5-8		
4:9-13		

9. In the first temptation (*4:3*), the devil appeals to a human need. What is wrong with Jesus using his divine power to meet his legitimate needs?

Why is this a temptation?

⇣Further reflection:
Jesus quoted from Deut. 6:13 in his second temptation. Look at this verse and the context (6: 1-4). Which Principles (1-2) do these verses relate to from the study thus far? Why?

10. What are other legitimate human needs and longings that we are tempted to meet illegitimately (apart from God's purposes, design, and timing)?

11. In the second temptation (*4:5-7*), the devil is enticing Jesus to go for his own glory; to be the ruler of his own universe. What is the trade-off in order to get it?

⇣Further study:
Compare and contrast Jesus' temptation with Adam's temptation in the garden (Gen. 3).
1) Characters
2) Environment
3) Challenge
4) Result
How were their circumstances different? What were the contrasting responses?

12. In the third temptation (*4:9-11*), the devil uses Scripture to raise doubt in Jesus' mind about God's sovereign care and control over his life. Why does he try to tempt Jesus in this way? (Look up the Old Testament references: *Ps. 91:11-12; Deut. 6:16.*)

Summary:

Each of these temptations is an attempt to disconnect Jesus from his Father. Throughout the wilderness experience, Jesus, as a human, displayed His trust in God by submitting to what He knew to be true. This is only possible if you know God intimately. One way to get to know the Father better is through the practice of the spiritual disciplines.

"We all have dreams. But in order to make dreams come into reality, it takes an awful lot of determination, dedication, self-discipline, and effort." ***(Jesse Owens, 1936 Olympic Gold Medalist)***

Spiritual disciplines are practices exercised to enliven and strengthen your walk with God. They prepare and condition your soul/heart so God can teach you and change you from the inside-out. The spiritual disciplines by themselves do not change you. It is God, through the Holy Spirit that changes you. The Holy Spirit transforms you as you put yourself in a place of dependence on him through the disciplines. (See *Phil. 1:6* and *2:12-13* for this human-divine cooperation.)

13. What disciplines (see list on the following page) did Jesus exercise during this testing period? How did each discipline strengthen His capacity to resist the temptation and remain deeply connected with the Father?

"Sow an act and You reap a habit Sow a habit and You reap a character Sow a character and You reap a destiny." ***(Charles Reade, 19th Century British Author)***

14. Read *Luke 4:13*. What does this say about the devil? What does this say about your need to daily connect with the Father through the disciplines?

Spiritual disciplines (practiced individually and in the community of your church):

Solitude - the act of spending an interval of time away from the distractions and lures of everyday living.

Fasting - a voluntary abstinence from foods (or something else) in order to redirect our appetites and focus to our Lord, who ultimately gives us our daily bread and sustains our existence.

Prayer - personal conversation with and to God.

Journaling - getting real with God by recording our personal insights, experiences, challenges, and feelings.

Study and Meditation - actively reading, pondering, observing, interpreting, memorizing, and obeying God's Word for our whole life.

Confession - acknowledging our sin before God by opening ourselves to His gracious Spirit's change from the inside-out, and then turning from our sin toward God (Repentance).

Fellowship - sharing the power of the resurrected life (in word, attitude, and deed) with other believers.

Worship and Celebration - responding with thankfulness in heart, soul, mind, body, and song to the greatness of God.

Witness - bearing the good news concerning Jesus Christ in words and acts of mercy and kindness to those who have not trusted in Christ.

Further reflection:
Go to: www. renovare.org to see more information about spiritual disciplines. Which area from the Renovare web site is most practiced in your life and which is lacking? Why? Begin a holy experiment with God and allow more of yourself given over to Him by journeying into a new area of growth from the Renovare web site.

SPORT CONNECTION:

Definition: Sportsmanship is a matter of being good (character) and doing right (action) in sports."[2] The spiritual disciplines cultivate good character so that we can act rightly and relate well in sport.

15. Review the **Temptations** in the chart on page 92.

Sport Temptation
Identify and record a temptation specific to your sport world that relates to each temptation in this passage.

Truth
What would be a biblical truth to "pull down" (see list on page 68 for some personal examples) at that moment to overcome the real temptation for you?

Spiritual Discipline
What spiritual disciplines off the field would help prepare you for a godly response to that temptation in your sport-specific situation?

(For example, you may be tempted to prove your worth and value (**Sport Temptation**) *by spending an extra hour in the gym everyday or some other kind of additional workout. Of course, this may be necessary to improve your skill level, but your work-ethic should flow from the* **Truth** *that you are accepted, adequate, and loved (see 1, 3, 19 on page 68) so you don't need to earn your value and worth by working out longer to keep yourself, the coach, the team or someone happy. A* **Spiritual Discipline** *like reading God's Word and confessing this wrong thinking would help bring experiential truth* (**Inside Game**) *to change your perspective about yourself, your practice routine, and your way of relating to others and God.)*

16. How is Satan challenging your view of God, winning, losing, your opponent or yourself?

What lies do you sometimes believe about yourself in sport?

What would help give you confidence and authority so that you strongly oppose this temptation to yield to Satan?

17. How do you understand the famous quotation by Grantland Rice? Agree or disagree? What would be some of the implications of this in your pursuit of winning as a Christian?

"When the one Great Scorer comes to mark against your name, He writes not that you won or lost but how you played the Game."
(Grantland Rice, 20th Century Sportswriter)

P|3
C|3

"The correct practice of sport must be accompanied by practicing the virtues of temperance and sacrifice; frequently it also requires a good team spirit, respectful attitudes, the appreciation of the qualities of others, honesty in the game and humility to recognize one's own limitations. In short, sports, especially in less competitive forms, foster festive celebration and friendly coexistence. While playing sports, Christians also find help in developing the cardinal virtues—fortitude, temperance, prudence and justice."[3]
(Pope John Paul II)

Putting It Together: JUST DO IT

God cares enough for His people that He chose tangible symbols or images like a rainbow, a cross, a cloud by day, and a pillar of fire by night to remind His children of His promises, power and presence. These concrete reminders (**Truth**) influenced the way God's people saw and interpreted their daily, life experiences.

"One man practicing good sportsmanship is far better than 50 others preaching it."
(Knute Rockne, former Head Coach Notre Dame)

In the same way, we can appropriate symbols that enable us to properly evaluate our life and sport experiences. A practical way to focus and to apply the truths learned is through the use of such notes or reminders, called "focal points."

Focal points are visual reminders (and verbal reminders) that God is your Audience, with God's Spirit empowering you to be rightly motivated as you compete—**practicing the presence of God in sport.** The intentional use of a focal point is a spiritual tool that you can use to re-train yourself to see sport and life as God-intended.

How does it work? "Down-Time is His Time"

Every sport has certain "**down-times**" (i.e. time-outs, change of possessions, half-time, etc.) built into the game itself. This "**down-time**" is His time which can be used instantaneously to reflect on your (**focal point**) and remind you why you are even competing. Technically, every minute is God's time but you can seize a short pause in the game, if need be, to re-focus your attention and re-direct your efforts. This is not to interfere with things like the game or your coaches instruction. You decide how to best use a down-time with respect to the other game variables. Keep this simple and practical so that you do not become mentally paralyzed. This should be a help not an hindrance. At first, it is like learning to ride a bike, methodical and slow. Over time, this tool can become second nature so that it becomes a part of your game day ritual.

You can begin your practices or competition by selecting some kind of visual reminder (**focal point**) to help you refocus when your attitude is skewed, your intensity wanes, or you lack mental concentration. Pick something natural, a part of the game or field of competition that will help you remember you are competing in that sport as an instrument for God's glory. For example, the lines on a track, field, or court serve as the defining boundaries of the game. These lines, as a focal point, could remind you that you are bounded by God's love and acceptance, for He defines your value and worth. Be creative but committed to give this a try.

Pre-game Plan:
- Pick a Focal Point
- Why this one?
- How does it remind you of God's truth (His promises)? (see page 68)

If you find yourself struggling during the heat of competition, take a "**down-time**" moment—positive self-talk (not to distract you from the actual game)— to quickly see the line (**focal point**) and re-focus your attention and energy to the game at hand.

Game-Process: [4]
- After some incident/event

↓
- **Relax:** Deep breath (it's okay!)

↓
- **Down-time** moment (find a pause in the game)

↓
- **Re-focus Attention:** Focal Point

↓
- **Re-direct Thoughts:** Remember what is true about you as a Christian.

↓
- **Re-channel Effort:** Apply God's truth to the situation and allow His Spirit to empower you from the inside-out to the effort at hand.

For a variation, try thinking of a verbal reminder that refocuses your attention on Christ at that particular time. More will be said about this in the next chapter.

GOD CONNECTION:

18. Journal your thoughts about God, Satan and yourself. What do you need to think and do as a result of this study?

19. Look through the list of spiritual disciplines. What disciplines do you need to start in order to "train for godliness?"

    How will you begin to do that this week?

DAILY CONNECTIONS

Day 1

In the study, we learned that metaphorically the desert represents "a place of solitude and barrenness where all of one's comforts are stripped away." It is no coincidence that Satan chooses this point in Jesus' life to attack with temptations. We can be most susceptible to sin when we are at an unstable, precarious, or troubling time in our lives. Satan will try to exploit these opportune moments to lead us away from our obedience to God.

Draw a brief timeline of your life, charting several of your best times or highest points, as well as some of your worst times or lowest points. Pick one or two of the low points, or deserts, and begin to remember the circumstances at that time in your life. Identify the key people, experiences, emotions, etc. that contributed to making this a tough period. In what ways did Satan tempt you during this ordeal? What lies did he try to make you believe about yourself? How did you respond to these situations? In what areas did you have victories, and in what areas did you succumb to temptation? How would you hope to respond differently to those same temptations today? What specific truths would you speak to yourself to combat Satan's lies?

Day 2

Galatians 6:1-2 says, "Brothers, if someone is caught in a sin, you who are spiritual should restore him gently. But watch yourself, or you also may be tempted. Carry each other's burdens, and in this way you will fulfill the law of Christ." (*NIV*)

God gives us Christian community as another means to fight the temptation of sin. We are called to help fellow brothers and sisters with their transgressions by carrying their burdens. This means asking questions about areas of their lives they may be struggling in, listening when they need to talk or process what is happening, praying for them, encouraging them with love and Scripture so that they can overcome the sin, and reinforcing God's unconditional love and their identity as daughters and sons of the Father.

We are also called to be vulnerable and allow others to help us in these same ways.

Find a friend or group of friends that you can do this with on a regular basis. These should be people you trust, and who will listen and share God's perspective with you. Set up a weekly time to get together and "carry each other's burdens."

"To be a Christian without prayer is no more possible than to be alive without breathing."
(Martin Luther King, Jr.)

Day 3

One of the most important spiritual disciplines we can exercise is prayer. Prayer is talking with and to God. It is the medium that allows us to express our innermost desires, joys, praises, laments, sorrows, victories, and defeats. Through prayer, we have access to an intimate relationship with the God of the Universe. It is important, therefore, that we know how to pray.

A common acronym to help us practice this discipline is **A.C.T.S.** Let's examine this model closely and see how it applies to our personal prayer lives.

Further reflection: Praying the Lord's prayer before the game, taking a knee after a score, and huddling up to pray with the other team after the game, evidence the myriad of ways prayer is incorporated into sports. Should prayer be a part of sports? Should I pray to win? Is prayer in sports like prayer in schools? All these are important questions to be answered as Christians seek to integrate their faith and cultivate the spiritual disciplines in their sport and life.What are your thoughts on prayer in sport?

Adoration – Worship God and love Him with all of your heart, soul, and mind. Praise God for all of His divine attributes such as His love, wisdom, justice, etc. Focus on how these characteristics have impacted your life.

Confession – Bring all of your sin, defiance, and imperfection before God and allow Him to forgive and cleanse you of it. Release all of the guilt associated with these acts and accept God's unconditional love.

Thanksgiving – Thank God for all of the blessings he has put into your life. They can be specific and tangible things, such as overcoming an illness, succeeding in school, getting a job, etc. — or more abstract, spiritual things such as grace, freedom, purity, etc.

Supplication – Ask God for your needs and the needs of others. Ask Him to help transform you in areas of sin, ask for guidance in areas of uncertainty, ask for help in areas that you need it.

Ask all these things on the behalf of others as well. Present your requests to God for His intervention in your life and the lives of others.

Read Jesus' example of how to pray in *Matthew 6:9-13* and identify the above aspects in the prayer. Begin a daily discipline of incorporating these aspects into your prayers.

"We are what we repeatedly do. Excellence, then, is not an act, but a habit."
(Aristotle)

Day 4

If you remember from the study, sportsmanship involves both being a good sport and doing the right thing in sport. But this is not easy! In fact, the issues and questions about what is good and right are arguably complex— especially as you progress in your level of and years in competition.

A. Visit some Web sites for a sportsmanship code of ethics:
  a) http://www.charactercounts.org/sports/codes/codes.htm.
  b) Do a Google search ("sports code of ethics").
  c) Ask your school/team if they have a sports code of ethics.

Obtain one and review it with respect to how you should relate to the officials and your opponent. How does it compare to your team's actual practices? Be specific.

B. Why is this so important? Review the (**Sports Factoid**) as to the difficult times that many in sport are experiencing.

Sports Factoid:
From a 17-year study with 72,000 athletes from 9th grade through college level:
1) Athletes score lower than their non-athlete peers on moral development.
2) Male athletes score lower than female athletes in moral development.
3) Moral reasoning scores for athletes steadily declined from the ninth grade through university age, whereas scores for non-athletes tended to increase. [5]

"When you stand on the victory stand, you must be able to ask yourself, 'Did I win this medal?'"
(Kip Keino, Kenyan, Olympic Gold Medalist in the 1500 and the 3000-meter steeplechase, from a speech urging young athletes not to use performance-enhancing drugs.)

Day 5

If sportsmanship (see Definition, page 80) is essential to the success and future of fair competition for everyone, then as a Christian you have a tremendous opportunity to positively contribute to competition by modeling sportsmanship for the integrity of the game and your God.

Recently, the following sportsmanship ad was promoted: **"Be a Hero, little EYES are watching."**

A. What kinds of sportsmanship traits (e.g., respect, integrity, courage, kindness, good judgment, responsibility) are needed on your team in order for your team to be recognized as heroes? Why is this missing on your team?

"To dope the racer is as criminal, as sacrilegious, as trying to imitate God; it is stealing from God the privilege of the spark."

(Roland Barthes, 20th Century French Philosopher)

B. As a coach or as a leader on the team, discuss how you can demonstrate better sportsmanship toward the officials and your opponent. What traditions or practices can you continue or implement to exhibit sportsmanship?

C. What about your own life? Identify one sportsmanship trait that you would like fostered in your life. What makes it so hard to develop this trait?

D. What action steps (before, during and after competition) can you begin to take to see this developed in your life?

REMINDERS:

1. God's goal is for you to mature and become like Jesus Christ in how you relate to God, others and yourself in sport and life.

2. Christ, as led by the Spirit, modeled for us how to exercise the spiritual disciplines for transforming our character.

3. Change occurs not by trying in your own power but by trusting in the power of the Spirit who works through the God-given spiritual disciplines.

4. The spiritual disciplines cultivate good character so that we can act rightly and relate well in sport and life.

5. We can use (**focal points**) as reminders of our best motivation, God's truth that we are loved and accepted, so that we can compete and live with God as our Audience.

NOTES:

1. Dallas Willard, *The Spirit of the Disciplines* (San Francisco, CA.: Harper and Row, 1988), ix.

2. Russell W. Gough, *Character is Everything: Promoting Ethical Excellence in Sports* (Orlando, FL.: Harcourt Brace, 1997), 21.

3. Pope John Paul II, *Sports and Culture:Two Vital Forces for Mutual Understanding, Culture and Development among Countries* (September 27, 2004) Online; available from http://www.appleseeds.org/sports_virtue.htm [accessed 28 September 2005].

4. As Christians, we should be more in tune with the insights from sport psychologists. These insights when processed through a Christian grid can help us live more freely and sometimes (as studies indicate) perform better. However, the purpose of this exercise is not to idolize self or a win. It is to keep God at the center of what you think, say and do, which by the way can coexist with good results (no guarantee). *See* Robin S. Vealey, *Coaching for the Inner Edge* (Morgantown, WV.: Fitness Information Technology, 2005), 201-66.

5. L.A. Lowe, *Differential Moral Reasoning Outcomes Among College Student-Athletes as a Function of Athletic Participation at Division I and Division II Universities* (11 May 2004) Online; available from http://employment.education.uiowa.edu/lalowe/07c336_ePortfolio/Impact_Athletics_Coll_Stud.htm [accessed 30 September 2005]; Angela Lumpkin, Sharon K. Stoll, and Jennifer M. Beller, *Sports Ethics: Applications for Fair Play* (Boston, MA.: McGraw-Hill Education Publishers, 2003); http://www.educ.uidaho.edu/center_for_ethics/research_fact_sheet.htm.

RESOURCES:

Ken Boa, *Conformed to His Image.*

Darrell Bock, *Luke: Baker Exegetical Commentary on the New Testament.*

Craig Clifford and Randolph M. Feezel, *Coaching for Character.*

Jay Coakley, *Sport in Society: Issues and Controveries.*

Russell W. Gough, *Character is Everything: Promoting Ethical Excellence in Sport.*

Tony Jones. *The Sacred Way: Spiritual Practices for Everyday Life.*

Angela Lumpkin, Sharon Kay Stoll, and Jennifer M Beller, *Sport Ethics: Applications for Fair Play.*

Robert C. Roberts, *The Strengths of a Christian.*

George Selleck, *Raising a Good Sport in an In-Your-Face World.*

Robert L. Simon, *Fair Play: Sport, Values, and Society.*

Jim Thompson, *Positive Coaching: Building Character and Self-Esteem Through Sports.*

Gary M. Walton, *Beyond Winning: The Timeless Wisdom of Great Philosopher Coaches.*

Donald S. Whitney, *Spiritual Disciplines within the Church.*

Dallas Willard, *Renovation of the Heart.*

Dallas Willard, *The Spirit of the Disciplines.*

John M. Yeager, *Character and Coaching:Building Virtue in Athletic Programs.*

Temptation	Sport Temptation	Truth	Discipline
#1 Meet your own needs (Example)	Gamesmanship- gaining an edge by inappropriate actions and disrespectful attitudes toward the opponent.	Love/respect others (opponent) as you love yourself. (*Mk.12: 31*)	Spend time studying and meditating on God's Word so that you see everyone as worthy of God's love and respect, especially your opponent.
#2 Go for your own glory			
#3 Prove your own power			

"...Unlike college, where I was a starter, I sat on the bench all season. Despite appearances, it turned out to be a great year after all, because the struggles I went through drew me closer to Christ. He showed me that even Joseph [Genesis 37-50] spent some time in the pit before being raised up to the palace. So I figured the best thing I could do was work hard, stay humble, and wait on the Lord. My patience paid off..."
(Michael Redd, NBA Player, describing his rookie year with the Milwaukee Bucks.)

Media moment: Think back to Jim McKay on "ABC Sports," with his dramatic opening line —"Spanning the globe to bring you the constant variety of sport! The thrill of victory ... and the agony of defeat! The human drama of athletic competition! This is ABC's Wide World of Sports!" Wow, this is the power-packed glory of sports!

As an athlete or coach, you know that set-backs, defeats, injuries or bad calls are part of the game. How you handle these inevitable challenges will often determine the kind of person you will become both in sport and beyond.

Just as sports is not immune to hurt and pain so isn't the Christian life. As a Christian in sport, this life is not about "if" you will experience trials or painful circumstances but it is about "when". For you, the issue is more about how you will respond to and grow from the trial as a follower of Christ.

4

PRINCIPLE FOUR Chapter

Genesis 37-50 "The Story of Joseph"

Hurtin' for Certain

GOD ALLOWS PAIN AND TRIALS TO DEEPEN YOUR CHARACTER FOR HIM

Trials and suffering are part of God's game for molding and shaping us, as we see and respond appropriately.

Hurtin' for Certain

CONTEMPORARY CONNECTION:

Take a minute and plot your life on a timeline (include only the main high and low points of your life). How have these events affected your view of God and yourself? If appropriate and applicable, share with the group.

"Life is 10% of what happens to you, and 90% of how you respond to it."
(Charles Swindoll, Author and Pastor)

In the New Testament, James talks about trials and how we are to respond to them. Look at the text below and make a list of observations about trials and how we should respond to them?

"Consider it pure joy, my brothers, whenever you face trials of many kinds, because you know that the testing of your faith develops perseverance. Perseverance must finish its work so that you may be mature and complete, not lacking anything." (*James 1:2-4, NIV*)

"The ultimate measure of a man is not where he stands in moments of comfort, but where he stands at times of challenge and controversy."
(Dr. Martin Luther King, Jr.)

Describe some adverse experiences in your sport life that you viewed as bad or unfair. How did things turn out?

"Show me someone who has done something worthwhile, and I'll show you someone who has overcome adversity."
(Lou Holtz, retired NCAA Football Coach)

Do you still feel the same way about it? Why or why not?

Trials are a given fact of life. Let's look at some challenging trials in the life of an Old Testament character and how he responded to them.

HISTORICAL CONNECTION:

Genesis 12-50 chronicles the initiation (*Gen. 12:1-3*) and spread of God's favor/blessings upon His chosen people (Abraham, Isaac, and Jacob) and the beginning fulfillment of His promises to accomplish His gracious purposes of reconciling people (from every nation) to Himself (a covenant relationship) for His glory.

In *Genesis 37-50*, we witness the story of Joseph. Joseph's father, Jacob, had 12 sons through different wives, which only contributed to the sibling conflict and family dysfunctions. Joseph is the 11th born and the first from Jacob's favorite wife, Rachel. Hence, Joseph was Jacob's favorite son. This favoritism, coupled with Joseph's strong self-assurance, caused tension in his relationship with his brothers.

↓Further reflection: Read James 1: 12-15. What is the difference between trials (testing) and temptations? Look up these two words and their meanings in a commentary or at http://www.crosswalk.com.What is God's purpose for trials and Satan's purpose for temptations?

Our story begins in *Genesis 37* with Joseph as the favored son, getting honored by his father with a beautiful robe, for which his brothers despise him. To make matters worse, Joseph has two dreams that illustrate that his father, mother and brothers will one day be ruled by him. He goes to check on his brothers who are out tending sheep. His brothers' envy and hate give rise to a plot to get even with Joseph.

BIBLICAL CONNECTION:

Trial #1: Read *37:18-28.*

1. Record the action verbs that designate specifically how the brothers acted (see v. 23, 24, 25, 28) or planned to act (v. 18-20) toward Joseph. What do their actions and conversations (v. 26-27) divulge about their character and their plot?

2. If you were Joseph, what would you have been thinking and feeling in the midst of these circumstances?

3. Is God mentioned anywhere throughout this whole scene? Have you ever felt that God was absent or abandoned you when life was confusing or in the midst of awful circumstances? Explain.

Summary:

The brothers return home and tell their dad that animals killed Joseph (*37:29-36*). Joseph is now working for Potiphar, one of Pharaoh's officials, who gives Joseph charge over his house because of Joseph's excellent work (*39:1-6*).

Trial #2: Read *Genesis 39:7-23*

4. This scene is intertwined with a seductive, Hollywood-type temptation (v. 7-13) and a consequential trial (v. 13-20).

List all the unfair allegations and actions from the wife and Potiphar himself toward Joseph (v. 13-20).

5. After this event, what might an honest observer of Joseph's life be thinking about God at this point?

6. What is Joseph's response to this injustice (v. 21-23)?

7. What possible relationship is there between Joseph's response to this injustice and the nine explicit references to the activity of God (see v. 2, 3, 5, 9, 21, 23) in this scene?

8. Though Joseph did not have the support of his family, and he was living in a strange land in the grim conditions of a prison, he did have God's presence with him. What attributes of God are depicted in and through Joseph's circumstances (especially see v. 21-23)?

↓Further study: Overcoming temptation is not easy, especially in the area of sexuality. So many top leaders, celebrities and sport stars fall in this one area. For many, they lacked the forethought and resolve to resist. Joseph provides us with some practical ways to address and overcome sexual temptations. Read 1 Cor. 6:18. What does it say about this area of temptation? Examine how this command in 1 Cor. 6:18 is clearly applied in Joseph's life (Gen. 39: 6-12). What specific ways (v. 8, 9, 10, 12) did Joseph deal with this temptation?

What comfort are we to take from our relationship with God when life has come unglued?

Summary:

Two of Pharaoh's leaders are thrown in prison with Joseph (chapter 40), who both had similar, perplexing dreams (*40:9-19*). Joseph interprets the dreams: one will be restored and one will be killed. Joseph asked that he be remembered when they get out.

"All the world is full of suffering. It is also full of overcoming."
(Helen Keller)

Trial #3: Read *Genesis 40:9-23*

9. What do these verses tell you about Joseph's character?

- 40:6-7:

- 40:8:

- 40:14:

- 40:15:

Further reflection:
You may not have justice (life is unfair), understanding (nobody seems to care), or support (where is relief when I need it most?) but you have God. Is that enough?

"The one thing you can't take away from me is the way I choose to respond to what you do to me. The last of one's freedoms is to choose ones attitudes in any given circumstance."
(Victor Frankl, Auschwitz Concentration Camp Survivor)

10. Read verses 14 and 23 again. Describe the mood and your initial reaction to "but forgot him"?

11. How would you be tempted to respond to this trial? Why?

Summary:

Two full years go by. Pharaoh begins to have dreams that he can't understand. The cupbearer finally remembers Joseph, who is able to interpret the Pharaoh's dreams: 7 years of prosperity and then 7 years of famine will come upon Egypt. Joseph proposes that the nation store up food during the years of prosperity. Pharaoh sees Joseph's wisdom and makes him ruler over all of Egypt (41).

The severe famine brings people from surrounding countries to buy grain from Egypt. Ironically, Jacob gathers his sons (Joseph's brothers) and sends them to get grain. They approach Joseph but did not recognize him because it had been approximately 20 years since they had sold him. Joseph chooses to hide his identity and inquires about his dad and youngest brother, Benjamin (42-44).

⇣Further application: Look up 1 Peter 5: 6-10. Identify the exhortations and promises of God concerning the reality of suffering for us. How could this console and encourage you to respond to trials with humility and trust?

Joseph did not choose his circumstances but he did choose his response. He may have had heart-felt questions, doubts, anger, fear… but he trusted God even if he didn't fully understand his situation. Why? It is not until chapter 45, when Joseph finally makes himself known to his brothers, and chapter 50, after Jacob died, that we get more clarity and resolution to why Joseph endured thirteen years of frustration and disappointment .

(Questions 12-16)

Most explanations we receive for why there is pain and suffering are often shortsighted because they lack the comprehensive and sovereign vision from God himself.

Read *Genesis 45:1-11* (especially v. 5, 7, 8) and *Genesis 50:15-21* (especially v. 19-21).

"What comes into our minds when we think about God is the most important thing about us... I believe there is scarcely an error in doctrine or a failure in applying Christian ethics that cannot be traced finally to imperfect and ignoble thoughts about God..."
(A.W. Tozer, 20th Century Pastor)

12. What emotions and attitudes are exhibited by Joseph during these two climactic scenes?

13. How is Joseph able to demonstrate this kind of affection and forgiveness toward his brothers' evil intent and actions?

14. What were God's purposes through this whole tragic-filled story? (Hint: there are multiple purposes woven throughout this drama.)

    What does this say about who God is?

Further discussion:
Bad things happen to people everyday. What are some of the normal responses toward and questions about God that people have after a difficult, painful or tragic event? Why these questions and responses?

15. How do these purposes relate to an underlying theme of Genesis and the whole Bible for that matter? (Look back over the first paragraph in the (**Historical Connection**) on page 98.)

How do you relate this all to what Jesus did and experienced on your behalf at the cross?

16. If a hurting and doubting friend declared the following exclamations and question (see below) about God in the midst of suffering, what have you learned from the Joseph story (the whole Bible study) that would incline you to genuinely hear your friend's pain and offer a godly perspective like Joseph?

- *"How do I make sense of this if God is suppose to be so loving?"*
- *"God must not care or want my best!"*
- *"God must not be good enough nor powerful enough to prevent my suffering!"*

↓Further study: Suffering greets us with many faces and leaves us with a host of "why" questions. Its pain often hinders our determination to live fully and responsibly. Cross-reference the following verses:
- Rom. 5:3-5
- Rom. 8:28
- Phil. 1:29
- 1 Pet. 1:6-7
- 1 Pet. 2:21
- 1 Pet. 4:19

How do these verses expand your understanding of the nature and purpose of suffering?

"In every sport there comes a moment when a spell of bitter weeping seems like a fair recess from whatever tough work is going on. It's only the steeliest among us who can fight the urge to turn negative--who instead will make contact and redouble her efforts. Call it grace under pressure. Call it grit... call it excellence."
(Susan Casey, Editor of *Sports Illustrated for Women*)

SPORT CONNECTION:
Joseph was subject to a range of trials and disappointments: Hated, envied, and rejected by his brothers, forgotten by the cupbearer, treated unfairly by Potiphar, seduced by Potiphar's wife, separated from his father and family, a murder attempt on his life, sold into slavery, thrown into jail, fabricated charges and false allegations brought against him, relocated to a foreign land where a different religion was prominent, and left to die.

As an athlete or coach, we will probably never come close to these kinds of trials but competition itself presents you with its own kinds of challenging circumstances and trials.

P4 C4

17. List 5-10 expected trials in competition with respect to the following relationships within sports: the game, the officials, the opponent, the team, your body, the player-coach relationship, the media/fans and the profession of sports.

18. Re-read *Genesis 50:20*. How could this view (or purpose from the Joseph story–see Q.14) help you to properly deal and respond to your list of expected trials from question Q.17? List some specific ways. What do you think about Dot Richardson's perspective as it pertains to this study?

"In sport, part of the game is accepting the umpire's call, no matter how hard that might be. Sometimes the calls go your way, and sometimes they don't."

(Dr. Dot Richardson, Two-time Olympic Softball Gold Medalist)

19. Many athletes think that God is most glorified when they are starting, winning or an All-American. What is flawed with this thinking? How can God be glorified while you are injured, on the bench or having a losing season?

20. Throughout the history of sports, athletes and coaches at all levels have experienced agony, defeat, and pain in sports or in their personal lives.

Review the chart on the next page for some of those trials in sports.

Record your immediate response to those ugly moments, and then ponder a godly, just response for one or more of those challenging injustices or personal trials. Which one most tests your faith? Why?

Athlete or Coach	Trial in Sports or Personally[1]	Response and Achievement
1. Many African-American Athletes in the 20th Century: Leon Day, Buck Leonard, Lucy Diggs Slowe, Hilton Smith, Josh Gibson, Ora Washington, Cool Papa Bell, Jackie Robinson, Jessie Owens, Alan Page, Art Shell, "Major" Taylor, Alice Coachman, Lee Elder, Eddie Robinson, and many others…	•Racist jokes and slander •Bigotry •Discrimination •Less than 5% of African-Americans, hold key management positions in professional and college sports	•First African-American in MLB: "He struck a mighty blow for equality, freedom, and the American way of life. Jackie Robinson was a good citizen, a great man, and a true American champion." (President Ronald Reagan, presenting the Presidential Medal of Freedom to Robinson's Family).[2] • Jesse Owens' and Luz Long's (German athlete) friendship defied Nazi racism in the 1936 Olympics in Berlin, Germany. [3]
2. Women during the 20th Century: Alice Coachman, Helen Mills Moody, Glenna Collett Vare, Gertrude Ederle, Althea Gibson, Kitty O'Neal, and many others…	•Sexism •Ridicule •Discrimination •Sexual Harassment	•Wilma Rudolph in the 1960 Olympics overcame segregation and polio. •Mildred "Babe" Didrikson Zaharias multi-sport phenomenon. •Women and men who struggled for the 1972 Title IX Legislation.

Athlete or Coach	Trial in Sports or Personally[1]	Response and Achievement
3. Michael Jordan	•Cut during his sophomore year in high school	One of the greatest NBA players ever
4. Peggy Fleming	•Pushy mother; age 13 her coach was killed in a plane crash	1968 Gold Medalist Figure Skater
5. Kip Keino	•Mother died prematurely; father was absent; abused by relatives	Kenyan Gold Medalist in Track (1968 and 1972 Olympics)
6. Pele	•Unable to buy soccer shoes; desired to meet his father's dreams	One of the greatest soccer players ever
7. Courtney Kupets	•Tore Achilles tendon at 2004 World Championship	Recovered from injury in time for 2004 Olympics (Silver and Bronze Medalist in gymnastics)
8. Gordie Howe	•Ridiculed by father; 9 kids in family; poverty	4 Stanley Cup Championships in Hockey
9. Tony Dungy	•First-born son, James, committed suicide	Faced this challenge with genuine grief and hope in His God, as a coach, husband, and father.

Note:
1) Evil injustices and inequities have plagued the history of sports like the rest of life, and as Christians, we (like Joseph) should become agents of God's goodness who work toward redeeming these perversions and atrocities.
2) Not every situation in this life is a success story (see Hebrews 11: 13-15, 39-40) which requires hope and a persevering faith in God, nor is every outcome in sports a God-honoring achievement.

Putting It Together: JUST DO IT

You have a choice to be either *bitter* or *better* by the trials or bad calls that you experience in sports/life.

"There is no attribute more comforting to His children than that of God's sovereignty. Under the most adverse circumstances, in the most severe trials, they believe that sovereignty has ordained their afflictions, that sovereignty overrules them, and that sovereignty will sanctify them all. There is nothing for which the children ought more earnestly to contend than the doctrine of the Master of all Creation--the Kingship of God over all the works of His own hands--the throne of God and His right to sit upon that throne."

(Charles Spurgeon, a 19th Century English Preacher)

This study liberates you to properly see and respond to your trials so that you can maintain a right focus and intensity in and through the trial.

However, sometimes we mess up by thinking and saying things in the "heat" of competition that are disrespectful to God and others.

What can you do?

A helpful exercise when you make a mistake is to mentally remember and verbally tell yourself (self-talk) "**nail it**" and then "**press on**".

Nail it - confess it to God, claim His forgiveness, walk by faith and be filled by the Holy Spirit. Even if your mistake is not spiritual this is still a helpful tool to console yourself in the midst of a game.

- A verbal reminder (**focal point**) to re-focus your attention, re-direct your thoughts, and re-channel your efforts to the situation at hand (see page 83).

- Hint: Say "nail it" when you make that spiritual blunder, or as a practical reminder if you make a mistake in the game itself.

Press on - press on (in the game) toward maturity in Christ even as you face and endure personal mistakes and trials.

- Another verbal reminder to yourself to re-direct your thoughts and attitudes back to Christ.

- Hint: Say "press on" in your heart and mind and then move on immediately with the game.

GOD CONNECTION:

21. Our trust does not need to be based on our circumstances, but on God's character. Identify 5 character qualities about God.

Which characteristics do you need to cling to during difficult times?

22. God is more concerned about your character than He is about your comfort. As you think about the difficulties in your life, consider God's purposes and Joseph's faithfulness in the midst of pain and trials. What changes need to be made in your attitude toward God or your actions toward others "so that you may be mature and complete, not lacking in anything?" Journal your thoughts.

23. Read the quote in the side-bar on page 108 by Charles Spurgeon. In addition to this quote, look up a few verses concerning God's sovereignty: *Ps. 103:19; Acts 17:24-28; 1 Tim. 6:11-16.* Why is it so important to be firmly convinced of this attribute of God? What might happen if you were not firmly convinced of God's sovereignty when you encountered pain, suffering and trials?

P|4
C|4

"God whispers to us in our pleasures, speaks [to us] in our conscience, but shouts in our pains: it is His megaphone to rouse a deaf world."
(C.S. Lewis)

Further reflection:
No one (not even God's children as seen in the Joseph story) is immune from pain and suffering in this life. Why is this so? Read C.S. Lewis' quote and discuss how his perspective enlightens your understanding of God. Do you agree or disagree?

DAILY CONNECTION:

Day 1

In today's study, we learned that although we cannot always control the circumstances around us, we are still responsible for how we react to trials. Think back to some competitive situations (practice, game, recreation) you've been involved in lately. How did you respond when a referee or player made a bad call against you? How did you respond when you or your team was playing poorly?

In what ways were you disappointed with your reactions? Oftentimes we cannot achieve our desired response in a situation until we have dealt with the belief systems that cause us to think and act in a certain way. If we believe that life is always fair and that we can dictate how situations around us will unfold, then when we don't get what we think we deserve, we will feel wronged by God and everyone around us. How did Joseph view trials? What role did he see God as playing in his trials? How would an understanding of trials as a part of God's sovereign plan for your life change the way you respond? How do you need to change your reactions to bad calls or poor performance in your sport? What might you learn in the midst of these ordeals?

For a mature perspective, see Michael Redd's quote below. How did he maintain a positive outlook?

> "...Unlike college, where I was a starter, I sat on the bench all season. Despite appearances, it turned out to be a great year after all, because the struggles I went through drew me closer to Christ. He showed me that even Joseph [Genesis 37-50] spent some time in the pit before being raised up to the palace. So I figured the best thing I could do was work hard, stay humble, and wait on the Lord. My patience paid off..."
>
> (Michael Redd, NBA player, describing his rookie year with the Milwaukee Bucks.)

Day 2

Read the following account of the refinement process of silver:[4]

As the silversmith goes to prepare his silver he holds only a lump of ore which is intermingled with bits of silver. In order to purify it, he must use intense heat. With the chunk of ore on his worktable, he begins the purifying process by building a fire to the right temperature, and places the hammered chunks of ore into a pot called a crucible. The crucible is then placed over the fire. As the substance softens and melts, the heavy silver sinks toward the bottom and the impurities (dross) rise to the top where the refiner removes it. He faithfully repeats this process by carefully watching, waiting and then removing the crucible and skimming the dross from the top. As he places it back in the fire, he turns up the heat. All the while, the refiner never leaves the crucible. "How does the refiner know when the silver is ready? ...There is a dramatic moment when he knows that all the dross has gone from it. Peering over it, the silver suddenly becomes a liquid mirror in which the image of the refiner is reflected. Then he knows that his task is done."[5]

"There has never been a great athlete who died not knowing what pain is."
(Bill Bradley, U.S. Senator and former NCAA Basketball and NBA Player)

This passage is a beautiful allegory for the way God works in our lives through trials. Let's analyze the specifics and look for His reflection or meaning for us in our trials. When you relate the above story to your own life, who is the refiner? What do the impurities and tiny bits of silver represent? How does the process of refinement relate to what you experience during trials? What does the pure silver represent at the end of the process?

Now relate this process to an actual trial you have experienced. Draw parallels at every part of the process and describe how God refined you through your trial.

> "The beauty of the soul shines out when a man bears with composure one heavy mischance after another, not because he does not feel them, but because he is a man of high and heroic temper."
> (Aristotle)

Day 3

When applying the principles from these studies, it often helps to see real life examples of the issues being discussed. When we observe the way others react in certain situations, it can help us reflect on our own responses in similar settings. Watch a competitive game of some kind (high school, college, pro; in person, on TV; it doesn't matter as long as it is an intense contest).

Using the table below, chart the reactions of the **Athletes** and **Coaches** to bad calls or tough breaks throughout the course of the game. In the **Activating Event** column, describe the trial the athlete or coach faces: a bad call by a referee, an injury, a run by the other team, etc. In the **Actual Response** column, describe how the player or coach responds to the trial: What emotions dominate their response? Do they remain calm or become flustered? Are there changes in the athlete's ability to perform? In the **Best Response** column, apply what you have learned from the studies so far and suggest ways in which the athlete or coach may have responded better.

Athlete or Coach	Activating Event	Actual Response	Best Response

While filling in this last column on the previous page, think about Joseph's reactions to those around him and to God in the midst of all of his struggles. How would viewing God as sovereign and not pursuing revenge or retaliation against those who have wronged you influence the way you react on the field of play?

> "Always seek out the seed of triumph in every adversity."
> (Og Mandino, Author)

Day 4

Joseph understood that God was the source of his abilities and opportunities. He knew that it was by God's grace, and not his own doing, that he could interpret dreams, manage people, and interact with high-ranking Egyptian officials. Subsequently, Joseph was able to view every trial the same as every blessing—an opportunity to worship the Lord. He remained faithful while in slavery and prison, always glorifying God with his talents through his effort and hard work. When it came time for Joseph to go before Pharaoh, he refrained from exalting himself and gave God the glory for his ability to interpret dreams (*Gen.41:15-16*). After becoming Pharaoh's right-hand man, Joseph serves his family and others from his position of influence by storing up a supply of grain so that they may eat during the 7-year famine.

What abilities and opportunities has God blessed you with? How have you tried to glorify him with these gifts?

> "When you face disappointments and obstacles in life—such as the injuries I've suffered this year—it's easy to give in to anger, frustration, and disappointment. I'm not saying I haven't experienced those feelings, but I don't allow them to take my focus off God's purpose, which is much bigger than anything I could conceive. My role on this team isn't about me; it's about God and what He's doing through my life. Knowing He is in control has given me peace. In fact, my injuries have actually caused my faith to grow."
> (Josh Williams, NFL Player)

Are you more likely to be faithful with your blessings in times of trial or abundance, and why? In whose lives do you have a position of influence? What are ways you can use your unique gifting to serve these people and others? Identify some people closest to you and reach out to them with your God-gifted influence.

Day 5

After his interaction with Pharaoh, Joseph becomes a very powerful man. He now has an opportunity to repay his brothers for selling him into slavery. Instead, Joseph not only lovingly forgives his brothers, but views their selling him into slavery as a God-ordained means for him to serve them (*Gen. 45:4-11*). Joseph rightly chooses reconciliation over revenge.

Think of someone with whom you have unresolved conflict. This can be someone you hurt, who hurt you, whom you have been in a fight with, jealous of, bitter towards, etc. Seek reconciliation with this person. Go to them and apologize for any ways in which you have wronged them, then in a non-accusatory way, honestly tell them ways in which they have hurt you. Accept any apologies they offer and begin to forgive them. Throughout the process, genuinely try and show to them the same love and grace that Joseph displayed to his brothers.

"Life is never easy, but the struggle you go through is always worth it, and in the end it makes everything so much greater... God is always there, and there is a purpose for everything that happens."
(Courtney Kupets, 2004 Olympian who overcame an injury at the 2004 World Championships shortly before competing in the Olympics.)

REMINDERS:

1. Trials are a given in sport and life, and they come in all shapes and sizes—never good timing for athletes and coaches.

2. God's goodness takes into account the messy nature of pain and trials in order for you to grow in your trust of Him and His purposes for you.

3. God desires to use you when others would give up on, quit or forsake sport and life.

4. In the midst of a trial, choose God's way of better over bitter so that you can speak hope into the chaos and crises of others in sport and life.

5. In the highly-charged sports world, sometimes our spiritual defenses are down so we spiritually stumble and sin. You can recover by genuinely "**nailing it**" and "**pressing on**" with the goal of re-focusing your attention and efforts to God's purposes for sport and life.

NOTES:

1. Michael Clarkson, *Competitive Drive* (Champaign, IL.: Human Kinetics, 1999), 94-95.

2. Ralph Wiley, "Saviors," in *The Gospel According to ESPN: Saints, Saviors, and Sinners*, ed. Jay Lovinger (New York: Hyperion, 2002), 172.

3. For the Jesse Owens' story, *see* the Web address http://www.charactercounts.org/sports/Olympic/olympic-report-ethicssportsmanship.htm.

4. Kay Arthur, *As Silver Refined: Learning to Embrace Life's Disappointments* (Colorado Springs, CO.: Waterbrook Press, 1997), 1-8.

5. Alan Robinson, "God, The Refiner of Silver," *Catholic Biblical Quarterly* 11, (1949), 190.

RESOURCES:

The Book of *Job* in the Old Testament.

Jerry Bridges, *Trust in God.*

Michael Clarkson, *Competitive Fire.*

D. Stanley Eitzen (ed.), *Sport in Contemporary Society.*

Peter Kreeft, *Making Sense Out of Suffering.*

Peter Kreeft, *Three Philosophies of Life.*

C.S. Lewis, *A Grief Observed.*

C.S. Lewis, *The Problem of Pain.*

Ravi Zacharias, *Cries of the Heart: Bringing God Near When He Feels so Far.*

"When I was going through my transition of being famous, I tried to ask God why was I here? What was my purpose? Surely, it wasn't just to win three gold medals. There has to be more to this life than that."

(Wilma Rudolph, 1960 Olympic Games, Track & Field. First American woman to win three gold medals.)

In sports, achievement is primarily measured and recorded by the scoreboard, stop-watch or the judge, depending on your sport. This is just how it works. However, these game evaluations or instruments are not perfect nor do they completely examine everything. "ESPN" highlights reminds us that sometimes the real winner failed to win because of a bad call, scoring malfunction, cheating, or the impropriety of a judge. Perhaps this is why we have instant replays, for we all want the true winner to be rewarded.

As a Christian in sport, we ultimately rely on God (as our Audience), who oversees everything from start to finish. Of course, that does not mean God steps out on the field to overrule some infraction or outcome, but it does mean that our striving to excel in competition is weighed and examined by God Himself. God has endowed you with His gifts and He cares how you responsibly play the game as His steward. Moreover, your experiences and efforts in sport are connected to the rest of your life roles. Even the NCAA implies this in their ads—most athletes "will be going pro in something other than sports." Therefore, God calls you to be an agent of change—"salt and light"—now in sport and beyond.

God desires to reward our faithful service in sport and beyond with His joyful presence at His glorious return. His victorious return assures us that there is victory beyond sport itself. He has secured our victory so that we can faithfully serve and affect change now and persevere toward His total and final victory.

5

PRINCIPLE FIVE Chapter

Matthew 25:14-30 "The Parable of the Talents"

Victory Beyond Competition

GOD'S PLAYING FIELD EXTENDS BEYOND YOUR COMPETITION

The return of the King calls us to be faithful stewards of our time, talents and treasures now in sports, as well as beyond.

Victory Beyond Competition

CONTEMPORARY CONNECTION:

Picture yourself walking through a cemetery after a funeral:

1. What kind of feelings, thoughts and experiences do you associate with a cemetery?

2. What are some similar characteristics of every gravestone?

3. Each gravestone represents a real life. What are some things people are often remembered for in this life?

"I love the game of basketball but it does not define me."
(Michael Redd, NBA Player)

"My whole life I had a carrot to chase... for 16 years, winning the Super Bowl was my carrot. Everything revolved around that. All of a sudden there's no carrot anymore, and you start wondering what you're going to do with your life. You play golf or you try business stuff, but it's not even close. You end up spinning yourself like a tornado..." [1]
(John Elway, former NFL Player)

4. Compare the two athletes' comments in the side-bar. What do these candid comments teach you concerning the different things people are living for now?

After death, in retrospect, most people wanted their lives to matter, to amount to something. Who and what they lived for is summed up by the hyphen on their tombstone between the DOB and DOD. In many ways, the kind of life you lived depends on how you live the hyphen. It's obvious that we don't remember all of the facts and statistics of each person. They are short-lived. But what about how they lived their lives? What will be remembered, and who will remember them?

HISTORICAL CONNECTION:

In Matthew 24, as Jesus is personally preparing for his own death, he is also teaching his disciples one last time about what is going to happen between his first and second coming. He fills their minds with pictures of future wars and calamities that the world has never known, but in the end and at the proper time, He will come back as the King of the universe (*Matthew 24:29-31*). He then tells a series of parables (*24:32-25:30*), stressing different points of how and why they should live as citizens of His kingdom in light of His future return.

Kingdom of God - The Gospels (Matthew, Mark, Luke and John) announce that Jesus Christ, as prophesied in the Old Testament and fulfilled in the New Testament (*Mark 1:14-15*), is the bringer of God's rule and reign (kingdom) through His life, His teaching, His ministry, His death and His resurrection.

BIBLICAL CONNECTION:

Read *Matthew 25:14-30*

5. What are the three "acts" in this drama? Identify the characters and action of each scene.

a) 25:14-15:

b) 25:16-18:

c) 25:19-28:

Definition of terms:

The master gives each servant a portion of his goods before departing. He expects each servant to invest the talents. A talent is a unit of money, with each talent worth about 6,000 denarii. One denarius was equivalent to a day's salary. It would have taken a worker 20 years to earn one talent. The word "talent" has come to represent not only money but the abilities and gifts (personal resources) God has entrusted to His people (see the side-bar for application).

Further applicationn:
God has blessed you with talents/gifts and made you with a unique, particular S.H.A.P.E.
S-spiritual gifts
H-heart/passion
A-abilities
P-personality
E-experiences
Take a moment to share and/or record the characteristics for each letter in your S.H.A.P.E.[2]

6. Look at the references about the master in verses 14-15. What does this imply about him?

7. How did the master determine how much each servant received?

Record the answers in the chart (page 138) for questions 8-10.

8. What were the actions, motivations, and perspectives of each servant toward the master and his gifts? (Be specific)

9. How did the master reward them? Observe the master's words, conversations, commendations, invitations, criticisms, and evaluations.

↓Further study: In the book of Genesis (1-2), God created us in His image with the accompanying privilege and responsibility to cultivate His creation (called the "Creation mandate"). Read Gen. 1:27-29; 2:8, 15. What specifically is the task given by God? The purpose of this mandate is for all people to share in the development and management of God's resources on His good Earth. For example, some people invent, educate, manufacture, legislate, budget, build, market, sell, judge, doctor, police, paint, write, counsel, coach, and play, all for the sake of advancing culture.

10. As a listener to this story, how would you describe the character traits that are exhibited in each of the servants?

11. How are character, motivation and action related to the conception that each servant had of the master?

"Not only is there more to life than basketball, there's a lot more to basketball than basketball."
(Phil Jackson, NBA Head Coach)

12. The third servant was gripped by fear (v. 25), motivated by self-protection (v. 18, 24, 25), and disposed to laziness (v. 26), resulting in failed stewardship (responsibly using God's talents) What fears are preventing you from maximizing God's talents in your life?

13. In competition, what is the difference between "playing to win" or "playing not to lose/playing safe?" How about in life?

"Laziness may appear attractive, but work gives satisfaction."
(Anne Frank)

14. In the book of Proverbs, laziness or slothfulness is portrayed as a certain character type that is found on the path that leads to moral and spiritual failure. Look up some of the following verses: 12:11, 24, 27; 20:4; 21:5, 25, 26; 24:30-34; 26:13-16. What are some of your observations about this character type?

How do they complete your understanding of this vice called laziness?

Further study: The Parable of the Talents reminds us of this original commission (Genesis 1-2) and now, as salt and light (Matt. 5:13-16), Christians are to be faithful stewards by caring for and serving others on behalf of God. When we do this, we are identifying with God's kingdom and eternity.

Summary:

In many ways, this whole passage is a radical call to live as faithful disciples. Our lives should be characterized by a kingdom work-ethic, prioritizing and productively employing our efforts right now. We tend to become consumed by our sport (chapter one), and often it's not until we come to the end of our career that we begin to think beyond our athletic lives. Though sport is a valuable pursuit and endeavor, it is a subset of the kingdom of God, along with many other important roles and callings God has given to us (see chart on page 133).

"One isn't necessarilly born with courage, but one is born with potential. There is no greater agony than bearing an untold story inside you."
(Maya Angelou, Poet)

SPORT CONNECTION:

15. Tim McGraw's song, *Live Like You Were Dying*, narrates his dad's response to the news that his life would abruptly come to an end due to a terminal illness. Life teems with various ends: end of the day, end of a game, end of a relationship, end of a job, end of life, and the end of this Earth. This parable underscores a certain, impending end that should cause us to live differently today (**Eternal Perspective**).

"Nothing is more common than unfulfilled potential."
(Howard Hendricks, Teacher)

Eternal Perspective: "A prime mark of the Christian mind is that it cultivates the eternal perspective. That is to say, it looks beyond this life to another one. It is supernaturally orientated, and brings to bear upon earthly considerations the fact of Heaven and the fact of Hell." [3]
(Harry Blamires, Author and tutored by C. S. Lewis)

In the song, McGraw mentions the following changes were made in light of the impending end: "went skydiving," "went Rocky Mountain climbing," "went 2.7 seconds on a bull named Fumanchu," "loved deeper," "spoke sweeter," "gave forgiveness," "read the good book"… He asks himself, "What did I do with it?"; the reality that life is a gift that can disappear tomorrow. What do these kinds of changes indicate about how his dad was living his life before the news?

⇣**Further reflection:** (Read above quotes) Have you considered your own unfulfilled dreams, potential, and responsibilities? Will you daringly step out in faith as a follower of the Master/Christ so that you can fulfill His callings in your life (i.e., son, daughter, husband, mother, athlete, coach, father, student, business person, etc.)?

What kind of changes or adjustments to your (**Eternal Perspective**) do you need in sport and in life to "Live Like You Were Dying"?

How is your eternal perspective clarified by Jesus' final instruction and calling for everyone in Matthew 28:18-20?

16. "There are 360,000 NCAA student-athletes, and just about all of us will be going pro in something other than sports" (NCAA ad). If this fact is true, what are you doing now, as a good and faithful servant, to prepare for the future?

    Is there someone you can talk to about your service to God? Career?

"Life's most persistent and urgent question is, 'What are you doing for others?'"
(Dr. Martin Luther King, Jr.)

17. As an athlete or coach, like the servants, you have been entrusted with much. Using the chart below, list some of those "talents" and how you are responsibly using them to serve others (the key relationships) in your sport. Are you considering the physical, emotional and spiritual needs of those you influence?

Relationships	Talents: What? and How?
Coaches	
Teammates	
Trainer	
Athletic Director	
Opponent	
Other	

Further study:
Cross-reference: In 2 Tim. 1:14, Paul reminds us to "guard the treasure" which has been entrusted to us. Read through all of 2 Timothy and record the exhortations or commands given to Timothy. What is God saying to you regarding what you are to do with the treasure?

18. Our Master has not only entrusted us with skills and abilities for sport but there is a whole other world outside and beyond competition that equally needs God's attention, love and our responsible investment. List some of the social concerns and moral challenges that the nightly news or the daily newspapers report. How can you or your church (Christian ministry) serve to meet some of the social needs? How about as a team for a civic/social service project?

Putting it Together: JUST DO IT

"Most men lead lives of quiet desperation and go to the grave with the song still in them."
(Henry David Thoreau)

Sport is neither an escape from life nor is it all of life. With the Master's perspective, sport is an unbelievable opportunity to grow in your relationship with God and others and prepare you for life beyond sport. Sport, as a Christian, is situated within the context of the whole of God's kingdom in this life.

When sport is understood in the light of the largeness of God's kingdom, then you are able to invest immediately and faithfully in the lives of others both on game day and after the game. Your goal should be that others would consider and be drawn to your Audience of One—witnessed by your maximum motivation, character in Christ, response to trials and victory beyond competition.

↓Further reflection: (Read the above quote) The third servant in his desperation went to "the grave" with significant loss, like so many other men and women who sojourn on Earth. God has given you a divine song that is waiting to be sung through your sport, career, marriage, and family. Do you know your song? Are you singing it?

Pray that God would be pleased by your eternal perspective—kingdom focus and efforts. Tell someone about the life-changing message of God's good news concerning Christ Jesus. What an awesome privilege and responsibility to be God's ambassador in whatever role or calling He has you investing in for eternity.

"No matter what I face, I know God has a purpose and destiny for my life, that He has placed me here for a reason."
(Jeff Saturday, NFL Player)

God Connection:

19. Often, our actions are based on the way we perceive God. In other words, the one servant was fearful of his master so he was very cautious about his investment. Which servant can you most identify with? Is there anything God is asking you to do in which you are hesitant to respond faithfully? Why? Journal your thoughts.

Further study: Using a Bible dictionary or concordance, look up names of God in the Old and New Testaments. What aspect or image of God do you need to trust as you step out and invest your life?

Further reflection: Do you think God cares about your participation in sport? Why or why not? How might the Eric Liddell quote shed light on what matters to God in sports?

"I believe God made me for a purpose, but He also made me fast. And when I run, I feel His pleasure." (Eric Liddell, *Chariots of Fire*)

DAILY CONNECTION:

Day 1

The beginning of this study asks you to picture a cemetery and reflect on the things for which people are most often remembered. Sometimes you can get an insight into a person's life and what they were known for by reading the epitaph on the headstone. Epitaphs are usually fairly short, a couple of sentences at the most, and describe the way those closest to the deceased viewed them. They often focus on the impact a person had on those around them, what they were passionate about, possibly mentioning the roles through which they interacted with others. Here are some examples of real life epitaphs:

> *"He always stood for what was right and good."*
>
> *"Her true wealth was in her generous heart."*
>
> *"A devoted and loving wife and mother."*
>
> *"Here lies Ezekiel Aikle. Age 102. The Good Die Young."*

What do you want your epitaph to say? How do you want others to remember your life? What type of an impact would you like to have? The text that we read today is all about the ways in which you can invest your "talents" to make a difference for God's Kingdom. There are infinite ways for you to serve others and worship God while here on Earth, but you only have one life to invest.

On a 3x5 index card, write out what you would like written on your tombstone. Carefully consider the above questions. Make this a sort of vision statement for how you want to live your life. Put this card somewhere you will occasionally see it (the inside front cover of your Bible, on your bathroom mirror, in a journal, etc.), so that it can remind you of who you want to be and what type of an impact you would like to have on those around you.

Day 2

God has called us to different roles in this life. Some of our roles utilize our abilities to impact and serve our community and the world around us. Roles such as student, coach, athlete, teacher, lawyer, doctor, etc. enable us to use skills the Lord has given us to interact with lots of other people. These people (teammates, colleagues, employees, coworkers, clients) whom we interact with will all be able to observe the way we use our talents. We have a powerful opportunity to witness Christ's love and grace in our lives through everything from the quality of our work to how we deal with these people on a daily basis.

Other roles are narrower in their focus, in terms of with whom we interact. We are mothers, sons, sisters, boyfriends, wives, and friends. In these relationships we have an even larger influence and therefore responsibility. We can go a long way in shaping the lives of our family and friends. These people will see more closely the way we live and the things we value, and we will have many more opportunities to love and serve them.

In the chart on the next page, make a list of several roles to which you have been called to serve. Then next to each role, list different ways in which you can grow in these areas of your life. These can be ways in which you better love and serve people, ways you can become more effective in your job or sport, or ways in which you need to grow emotionally or intellectually. Take your newly formed list and make goals for each role that you play. Pray daily through these goals and ask God to help you be transformed in these different spheres of your life. Stay conscious of your goals and continually attempt to apply them to the living out of these roles.

"The secret of man's being is not only to live
but to have something to live for."
(Fyodor Dostoyevsky, Russian Author)

ROLES	GROWTH AREAS	GOALS

Day 3

Through the parable of the talents, Jesus wants us to gain a sense of urgency and importance in the way we go about living. We are to invest now and invest fully. Oftentimes, investing in God's Kingdom requires sacrificing earthly pursuits. We are to view our talents and abilities as truly belonging to God and therefore invest them in things that further His interests and not our own. Time and time again in the New Testament we read about people who cannot fully realize Christ's offer of salvation because they are grasping too tightly to wealth, power, status, and relationships in this world. They have used their blessings for personal glory and now do not want to use them selflessly. It is hard to let go of things that people have praised us for and to worship God as the center of our experience here on Earth.

Read *Philippians 3:4-11.* Paul was someone who was successful and praiseworthy. Go through verses 4-6 and discuss the significance of Paul's boasts.

> "We can't take any credit for our talents.
> It's how we use them that counts."
> (Madeleine L'Engle, Author)

What are some things that you can boast about?

Then Paul says something radical. In verses 7 and 8, he claims to consider all of his accomplishments and privileges now worthless. Why would Paul now consider these positives, "loss for the sake of Christ?" How could these things now hinder his relationship with God? How can the boasts you previously named potentially hinder your relationship with God? How can these abilities be redeemed and used to serve God selflessly?

Day 4

The term "calling" is often used to describe the way God brings someone into vocational ministry. The minister has been "called" by God to preach His Word as a profession. This is certainly one type of calling, but there are many others. As a matter of fact, God has multiple callings for each one of us. "Calling" can be defined as finding a need that you are uniquely gifted to fill. Similar to the parable, God has given us all talents and expects us to invest them in a wise way. Fulfilling these callings can come in the form of a job, a marriage, or serving others. Today, we want to focus on investing our talents to serve others who desperately need love and hope.

In order to find a need, you must be aware of what is going on in the world around you. Where are people suffering, being treated unjustly, starving, lost, depressed, etc.? What is the cause? How can you help change the situation? Helping those afflicted and oppressed is known as seeking social justice. Many Christians throughout the years have been champions of social justice. They have been faithful with their talents by investing them to help others overcome desperate situations. Some examples are Dietrich Bonhoeffer, Dorothy Day, Martin Luther King, Jr., Eric Liddell, Mother Theresa, Simone Weil, and William Wilberforce.

Read a biography on one of these people. As you read, think through why these people acted as they did. What did it have to do with their belief in God? How did they use their abilities to transform culture? What are ways in which you can act similarly in your culture?

Day 5

Because the Master's return is imminent and everyone is judged when He comes back, there is a daring challenge to get with it by investing NOW! A primary and general calling for all Christians is to invest their talents to share the good news of their salvation through Christ with those around them. If we truly believe that God exists, then we should be motivated to be His instrument of love and hope to others.

Make a list of people you know who do not have Christ's saving grace. Dedicate yourself to praying for them daily. Pray that God will change their hearts and allow them to experience His love. Pray that He will give you opportunities to share His good news with them. Pray for wisdom in discerning when those times are. Pray that you will always be a witness to the power and love of the Gospel.

REMINDERS:

1. Because God has endowed you with immeasurable purpose and talent, work and play with excellence.

2. Discover your SHAPE and your callings so you can faithfully exercise your talent in anticipation of God saying, "Well done, [my] good and faithful servant!"

3. Like the two good servants, invest your talents immediately, completely and faithfully on behalf of God and others.

4. Sport and life are gifts—they will expire some day, so live fearlessly and honorably.

5. Tell someone in word and deed about the life-changing message and love of Jesus Christ.

NOTES:

1. Rick Reilly, "Welcome to the Real World," *Sports Illustrated* 97, (7) (19 August 2002), 80.

2. Rick Warren, *The Purpose-Driven Life: What on Earth am I Here for?* (Grand Rapids, MI.: Zondervan, 2002), 227-40.

3. Harry Blamires, *The Christian Mind: How Should A Christian Think?* (Ann Arbor, MI.: Servant Books, 1978), 67.

RESOURCES:

David G. Benner, *Desiring God's Will: Aligning our Hearts with the Heart of God.*

Harry Blamires, *The Christian Mind: How Should A Christian Think?*

Stephen R. Covey, *The Seven Habits of Highly Effective People.*

Stan D. Gaede, *An Incomplete Guide to the Rest of Your Life.*

Patrick Morley, *The Rest of Your Life.*

John Piper, *Don't Waste Your Life.*

Quentin J. Schultze, *Here I am: Now What on Earth Should I be Doing?*

Gordon T. Smith, *Courage and Calling: Embracing Your God-given Potential.*

Rick Warren, *The Purpose-Driven Life: What on Earth am I Here for?*

Dallas Willard, *The Divine Conspiracy.*

	Action	Motivation	Perspective	Rewards	Character
Servant (5 talents)					
Servant (2 talents)					
Servant (1 talent)					

Sport Resources

Sport Ministry:

Athletes in Action (AIA)
651 Taylor Dr.
Xenia, OH 45385
937-352-1000
athletesinaction@aia.com

Christians in Sport
Frampton House
Victoria Road
Bicester
Oxford, ENGLAND
OX26 6PB
www.christiansinsport.org

Church Sport Recreation Ministry (CSRM)
5350 Broadmoor Circle NW
Canton, OH 44709
330-493-4824
www.csrm.org

Fellowship of Christian Athletes (FCA)
8701 Leeds Rd.
Kansas City, MO 64129
800-289-0909
fca@fca.org

360° Sports
PO Box 71776
Marietta, GA 30007
404-543-5579
info@360sports.net

Sport Organizations Committed to Good Competition:

Athletes for a Better World- www.aforbw.org
Canadian Centre for Ethics in Sports- www.cces.ca
CHARACTER COUNTS! Sports- http://www.charactercounts.org/sports
The Citizenship Through Sports Alliance- www.sportsmanship.org
Institute for International Sport- www.internationalsport.com/index.html
NAIA Champions of Character: A Character Development Initiative- http://naia.collegesports.com/champions-character
National Association for Sports Officials- www.naso.org
NCAA- www.ncaa.org
Positive Coaching Alliance- www.positivecoach.org
U.S. Office of National Drug Control Policy: Drugs and Sports- www.whitehousedrugpolicy.gov/prevent/sports/index.html
Winning with Character- www.winningwithcharacter.com/pages/program.html
Youth Sports- www.youth-sports.com

Christian Worldview Resources

Center for Bio-Ethics and Human Dignity- www.cbhd.org
Charles Colson's Breakpoint Ministry- www.pfm.org/
Internet Christian Library- www.iclnet.org/
Probe Ministries- http://www.probe.org
Leadership University- www.leaderu.com/

Contact Us

John White, Director of Sports Ethics
Athletes in Action, 651 Taylor Dr., Xenia, OH 45385

office: 937-352-1000
fax: 937-352-1121
email: **info@gamedayglory.com**

To order additional books, visit: **www.gamedayglory.com,**
or call: 937-352-1000. (Ask about quantity discounts.)

Speaking engagements:
John and Cindy White are available to speak to your sports team, organization, athletic department or coaching staff about the principles applied in this study. Presentations addressing the critical issues in sport for coaches and athletes can be customized to meet the needs of your particular group, and are available in seminar, conference or retreat formats.

Some of the most requested topics are:

Ethics in Sport…*Exercising a Christian Worldview in Sport*
Winning in Sport*…Competition, Celebration and Character*
Anger in Sport*…When anger becomes destructive*
Motivation in Sport*…Rising above fear, approval and status*
Anxiety in Sport*…Competing with joy and freedom*
Families in Sport*…Maintaining balance, purpose and success*

We would like to hear from you!
If you have benefited from this study, please tell us how. We are particularly interested in how these principles have shaped your understanding of and relationship with God in your sport experience. If you have any questions about practical applications in your sport, please write to us at info@gamedayglory.com. We would love to help in any way we can.

Are the Principles of *Game Day Glory* making a difference?
"Our desire at CCU is to see our student athletes transformed into stronger Christians, not just better players. *Game Day Glory* has helped us do just that. We took our whole department (coaches, staff, athletes) through the study and have seen God use it to help our athletes compete wholeheartedly and for a higher purpose."
Doug Yager,Director of Athletics, Colorado Christian University

For more information about Athletes in Action, visit www.aia.com.
For resources on Sports Ethics, visit www.aia.com/sportsethics/